Books by Eric Hammel

76 Hours: The Invasion of Tarawa (with John E. Lane)
Chosin: Heroic Ordeal of the Korean War
The Root: The Marines in Beirut
Ace!: A Marine Night-Fighter Pilot in World War II
(with R. Bruce Porter)
Duel for the Golan (with Jerry Asher)
Guadalcanal: Starvation Island
Guadalcanal: The Carrier Battles
Guadalcanal: Decision at Sea
Munda Trail: The New Georgia Campaign
The Jolly Rogers (with Tom Blackburn)
Khe Sanh: Siege in the Clouds
First Across the Rhine (with David E. Pergrin)
Lima-6: A Marine Company Commander in Vietnam
(with Richard D. Camp)
Ambush Valley
Aces Against Japan
Aces Against Japan II
Aces Against Germany
Air War Europa: Chronology
Carrier Clash
Aces at War
Air War Pacific: Chronology
Aces in Combat
Bloody Tarawa
Marines at War
Carrier Strike
Pacific Warriors: The U.S. Marines in World War II
Iwo Jima: Portrait of a Battle

Marines in
HUE CITY

A Portrait of
Urban Combat, Tet 1968

Eric Hammel

ZENITH PRESS

*This book is respectfully dedicated to all the men, women, and children who died in the battle for Hue,
and to all who still suffer from the wounds they sustained there.*

First published in 2007 by Zenith Press, an imprint of MBI Publishing Company, Galtier Plaza, Suite 200, 380 Jackson Street, St. Paul, MN 55101-3885 USA

Zenith Press titles are also available at discounts in bulk quantity for industrial or sales-promotional use. For details write to Special Sales Manager at MBI Publishing Company, Galtier Plaza, Suite 200, 380 Jackson Street, St. Paul, MN 55101-3885 USA.

To find out more about our books, join us online at www.zenithpress.com.

Editor: Scott Pearson

Designer: Tom Heffron

Printed in China

Library of Congress Cataloging-in-Publication Data

Hammel, Eric M.
  Marines in Hue city : a portrait of urban combat, Tet 1968 / Eric Hammel.
    p. cm.
  ISBN-13: 978-0-7603-2521-6 (hardbound)
  ISBN-10: 0-7603-2521-9 (hardbound)
1. Hue, Battle of, Hue, Vietnam, 1968. 2. Tet Offensive, 1968. 3. Urban warfare—Vietnam—Hue.
4. United States. Marine Corps—History—Vietnam War, 1961-1975. I. Title.
DS557.8.H83H364 2007
959.704'345—dc22

2006022062

On the cover: Marines from 1/5. *Bettman/Corbis*
On the frontispiece: An M60 machine gunner. *Official USMC Photo by Sergeant William L. Dickman*
On the title page: An Alpha/1/1 rifleman. *Official USMC Photo by Sergeant Bruce Atwell*
On the back cover: A Marine with a wounded Vietnamese girl. *Texas Tech Virtual Vietnam Archive/Douglas Pike Photo Collection*

Contents

Author's Note

I spent more than a year in 1989 and 1990 compiling as complete a narrative history of the battle for Hue as time, money, and a publishing deadline would allow. I spoke to nearly a hundred participants in the 1968 battle, including all three U.S. Marine Corps battalion commanders, many Marine staff officers, five of eight Marine infantry company commanders, and scores of junior leaders and troops of every type. The result was *Fire in the Streets: The Battle for Hue, Tet 1968.* The Marine Corps liked the book enough to place it, year after year, on the Commandant of the Marine Corps' professional reading list. I cannot guess how many Marines have read the book, nor how many I lectured on the topic of "military operations in urban terrain" over the years. Indeed, I delivered my lecture to Marines on the Marine Corps' last urban battle on the eve of Operation Iraqi Freedom.

The intimate narrative I produced as *Fire in the Streets* still stands. This is not an effort to supplant it, nor even to supplement it in a substantive way. This effort is a vehicle to show what urban combat *looks like,* using Hue as a relevant example. If this book has a theme, it is urban combat per se. If you look at the photos accompanying this volume's first chapter, then leaf through the pages with photos taken during the Hue battle, you will be struck at how similar many of them seem to be. If you then go online to http://www.usmc.mil and search the image archive there on such topics as "urban terrain" or "Fallujah," you will be struck once again by the way poses tend to repeat from World War II to Korea to Vietnam to Iraq. It's actually eerie.

I write military narratives to explain war to readers at a human level. Books with words have been a big part of my life, all my life. I put together one of them, *76 Hours: The Invasion of Tarawa,* with 250 photos and created *Bloody Tarawa.* The idea was to deepen my own understanding of war—words *and* pictures together. Then I went heavier with photos and captions in *Pacific Warriors* and *Iwo Jima.* Here now, because I already did the story in words, are mainly pictures. I believe that this book, *Marines in Hue,* stands alone in telling a particular story, and an enduring story, about a particularly vicious aspect of war. But it also fits hand in glove with *Fire in the Streets,* and experiencing both together might be something you'd like to try. Either way, this is about the aspect of human existence that has haunted a veteran's son from earliest memory: the face of war.

Eric Hammel
Northern California
Winter 2006

Acknowledgments

Above all, I wish to acknowledge and thank Colonel Chuck Meadows for the loan of his amazing personal collection of official and private photos taken in Hue. Chuck not only shipped this valuable collection to me for the third time in fifteen years, he also took time from his last 2005 visit to Hue to work his way through an ambitious shot list I gave him of important battle sites as they look today. Chuck would not hear of any form of compensation for his trouble on behalf of this project, so I wish to direct you to the very worthy cause at the root of his many trips back to Vietnam. Please visit http://www.peacetreesvietnam.org and read about the important life-saving mission to which Chuck Meadows devotes his life. If you approve of the work PeaceTrees Vietnam is doing, please support it in a meaningful way.

Other Hue battle veterans whom I wish to thank for providing photos for use in this volume are Alexander Kandic, Douglas Blayney, Dr. Jerome Nadolski, Richard Carter, Edward Neas, John Salvati, Tom Pilsch, and Chris Brown. Thanks, also, to Dick Wilkerson for providing personal photos from his visits to Hue and to combat photographer Bill Dickman for scouring his home for copies of photos he took in his official capacity during the battle.

For priceless help in accessing and scanning photos in official collections, I thank Theresa M. Roy and Donna Larker at the Still Pictures branch of the National Archives and Records Administration; Mike Miller, Pat Mullin, and Sue Dillon at the Marine Corps University Archive at Quantico, Virginia; Colonel Walt Ford at *Leatherneck* magazine; and Colonel Dick Camp and Lena Kaljot at the Marine Corps History Division.

I also captured many photos online from the amazing and thoroughly useful Texas Tech Virtual Vietnam Archive at http://star.vietnam.ttu.edu/starweb/vva/servlet.starweb?path=vva/vva.web. The photos from this rich source, which includes all U.S. Marine Corps Vietnam War command chronologies (and a lot more information as well), are used with permission.

Many thanks to Nancy Hoffman, of *Leatherneck,* for photographing yet another in a running series of portraits of the aging author.

Glossary and Guide to Abbreviations

A-1	Douglas Skyraider single-engine attack aircraft
AK-47	Soviet-pattern 7.62mm assault rifle
ARVN	Army of the Republic of Vietnam
CH-46	U.S. Boeing Sea Knight medium transport helicopter
DMZ	Demilitarized Zone
Duster	U.S. M42 tracked dual-40mm gun carriage
LAAW	U.S. M72 40mm light antitank assault weapon
LCU	U.S. landing craft, utility
M3A1	U.S. .45-caliber submachine gun (grease gun)
M4	U.S. Sherman medium tank
M14	U.S. 7.62mm assault rifle
M16	U.S. 5.56mm assault rifle
M26	U.S. Pershing medium tank
M41	U.S.-made ARVN Walker light tank
M42	U.S. tracked dual-40mm gun carriage (Duster)
M48	U.S. Patton main battle tank
M50	U.S. Ontos tracked six-106mm recoilless-rifle carrier
M55	U.S. quadruple-.50-caliber machine-gun truck
M60	U.S. 7.62mm medium machine gun
M79	U.S. 40mm grenade launcher
MACV	Military Assistance Command, Vietnam
MAF	Marine Amphibious Force
Mechanical Mule	Light cargo transporter, also used as a wheeled mount for 106mm recoilless rifles
Medevac	Medical evacuation
NVA	North Vietnamese Army
PBR	U.S. Navy Patrol Boat, Riverine
RPD	Soviet-pattern 7.62mm light machine gun
RPG	Soviet-pattern rocket-propelled grenade
SKS	Soviet-pattern 7.62mm bolt-action rifle
Skyraider	Douglas A-1 single-engine attack aircraft
VC	Viet Cong
VNMC	Vietnam Marine Corps

Maps

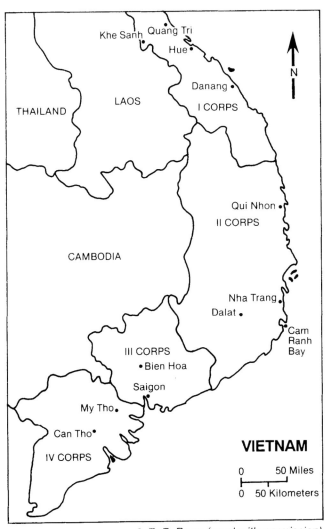

Khe Sanh   Quang Tri
Hue

THAILAND   LAOS

Danang

I CORPS

N

Qui Nhon

II CORPS

CAMBODIA

Nha Trang
Dalat

Cam
Ranh
Bay

III CORPS
• Bien Hoa

Saigon

My Tho

Can Tho

IV CORPS

VIETNAM

0   50 Miles

0   50 Kilometers

© F. F. Parry (used with permission)

I CORPS
TACTICAL ZONE

Miles   0   10   25   50

Kilometers   0   10   25   50

NORTH
VIETNAM

DMZ

South China Sea

QUANG TRI
Quang Tri

N

HUE
Phu Bai

THUA THIEN

Danang

QUANG NAM   Hoi An

LAOS

Tam Ky

QUANG TIN   Chu Lai

Quang Ngai

QUANG NGAI
XXX

II CORPS

CAMBODIA

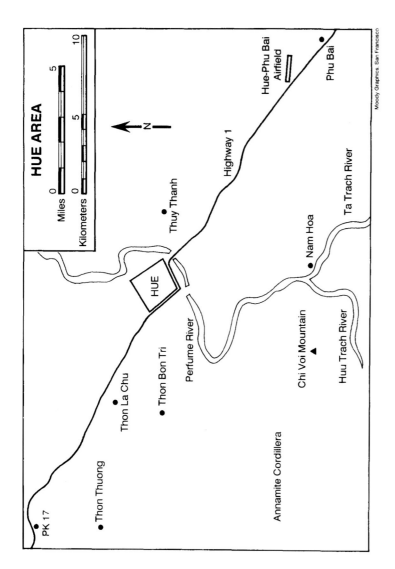

HUE AREA

Miles
0   5   10

Kilometers
0   5

Thon Thuong

PK 17

Thon La Chu

Thon Bon Tri

Perfume River

Annamite Cordillera

HUE

Thuy Thanh

Highway 1

Nam Hoa

Chi Voi Mountain

Hue-Phu Bai Airfield

Phu Bai

Ta Trach River

Huu Trach River

Moody Graphics, San Francisco

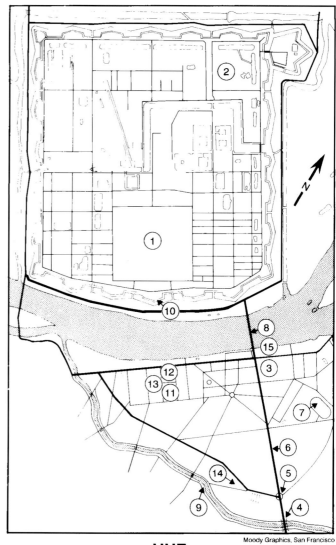

Moody Graphics, San Francisco

HUE

1. Imperial Palace
2. 1st ARVN Division CP
3. MACV Compound
4. An Cuu Bridge
5. Traffic Circle
6. Canefield Causeway
7. Tu Do Stadium
8. Nguyen Hoang Bridge
9. Phu Cam Canal
10. Citadel Flagpole
11. Thua Thien Provincial Prison
12. Thua Thien Provincial Admin. Center
13. Hue Municipal Power Station
14. Hue Cathedral
15. Doc Lao Park

Scale Tỷ lệ 1:12,500

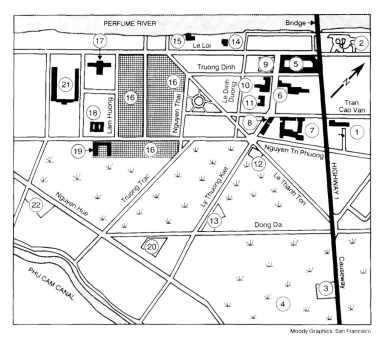

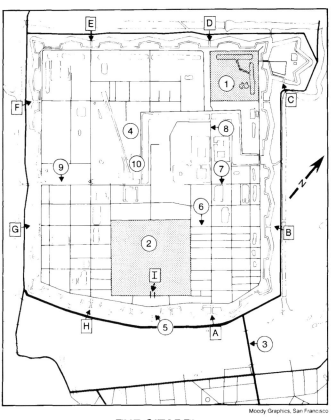

Moody Graphics, San Francisco

DOWNTOWN HUE

1. MACV
2. Doc Lao Park
3. Police Compound
4. Cane field
5. Hue University
6. Chemistry Lab and Music Room
7. Jeanne d'Arc High School
8. Le Loi Elementary School
9. Public Health Complex
10. Treasury
11. Post Office
12. Student Center
13. U.S. Consul's Residence
14. French Cultural Center
15. Cercle Sportif
16. Hospital Complex
17. Thua Thien Provincial
     Admin. Complex
18. Thua Thien Provincial Prison
19. Antituberculosis Center
20. U.S. Consulate
21. Hue Municipal Power Station
22. Le Lai Military Camp

THE CITADEL

1.	1st ARVN Division CP Compound	A.	Thuong Tu Gate
2.	Imperial Palace	B.	Dong Ba Gate
3.	Nguyen Hoang Bridge	C.	Truong Dinh Gate
4.	Tay Loc Airfield	D.	Hau Gate
5.	Citadel Flagpole	E.	An Hoa Gate
6.	Mai Thuc Loan Street	F.	Chanh Tay Gate
7	Tinh Tam Street	G.	Huu Gate
8.	Dinh Bo Linh Street	H.	Nha Do Gate
9.	Thuy Quan Canal	I.	Ngo Mon Gate
10.	1st ARVN Ordnance Company Armory		

Chapter 1

MARINES FIGHT IN CITIES AND TOWNS

The first time modern U.S. Marines fought in an urban landscape was on Saipan in mid-1944. The Marine Corps had no manuals, no doctrine, no plan, and provided no training for urban fighting. The Marines thrown into urban combat in the Pacific made it up on the fly, learning tough lessons in the tried-and-true Marine manner, through blood, bravery, and sacrifice. They took every urban objective assigned to them.

The Marine Corps undertook no post-mortems on city fighting after the Pacific War; it was as if it had never happened. No lessons learned were posted, few manuals were borrowed from the thoroughly experienced U.S. Army, no time was spent honing skills or developing standard techniques and equipment.

The next time U.S. Marines were called on to reduce an urban objective was early in the Korean War, at Inchon and Seoul, South Korea. It is likely that veteran urban fighters of the Pacific War took part, but the organization itself applied no formal training to securing these objectives. The fighting wasn't all that difficult in any case; the North Korean People's Army wasn't especially proficient in the defense and might have had less experience than Marines in urban combat.

There were no urban-type battles per se in the Marine Corps' resumé between late 1950 and early 1968. Veterans of urban combat certainly served in that period, and some rose to substantial rank, but they neither formalized nor shared their experiences. As an organization, the Marine Corps of January 1968 had no urban combat under its belt; it had no plan, no doctrine, not even a concept. What it did have were some very good, very smart warriors who were willing and able to do what U.S. Marines are expected to do—what they have always done—when faced with interesting and unexpected battlefield conditions—and that is muddle through as boldly as possible.

In a classic attack into urban terrain, the city or town is isolated around its periphery—to deny the defenders access to outside resources. Then it is typically "prepped" with artillery fire and air attacks. Shown here, Marine M4 medium tanks prepare to advance into cityscape. Naha, Okinawa, 1945. *Official USMC Photo*

Built-up areas are extremely difficult to picture from the ground. Buildings and hills often impede vistas, and the only open ground is often streets and roads, which defenders tend to stake out to get clear shots at attackers, who must cross them sooner or later. Weather permitting, American combat forces usually employ aerial observers to call in battlefield data from beyond the sight of troops on the ground. Aerial observers also direct air, artillery, and naval gunfire missions. Naha, Okinawa, 1945. *Official USMC Photo*

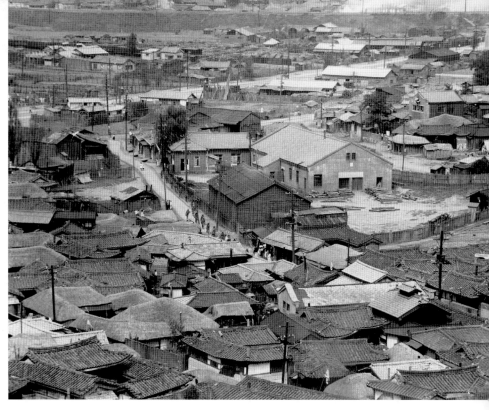

Even soldiers who grow up in cities don't realize how complex and vast urban terrain is until they experience the intensely Darwinian nature of combat there. Against a backdrop of buildings, roads, and fields running to the horizon in every direction, the platoon of Marines in the center of this photo is minuscule. If there are defenders hiding anywhere in this section of town, this platoon will be completely outclassed. Seoul, Korea, 1950. *Official USMC Photo courtesy of* Leatherneck

Armor is a mixed blessing in urban terrain. A tank can withstand all manner of fire while it stands off—or wades right in—to demolish buildings in the path of assaulting infantry, but it takes a lot of troops to defend a buttoned-up tank whose crew has extremely limited vistas. Moreover, tanks can be heard a long way off, and they tend to attract great volumes of defensive fire. Okinawa, 1945. *Official USMC Photo*

This Marine M26 tank would have a difficult time bringing its main gun to bear on targets on the ridge that dominates its route of advance. Note that the Republic of Korea and UN flags emblazon the building at top right. This, and flying white flags, are virtually universal gestures by residents who do not want to be mistaken for the losers of an urban battle. Seoul, Korea, 1950. *Official USMC Photo courtesy of* Leatherneck

The nature of even undisturbed urban terrain—block after block of individual buildings composed of one, two, or many levels of rooms separated by walls composed of everything from wood lathe to steel-reinforced concrete—tends to balkanize tactical units to their lowest common denominators. Leadership is often impossible to maintain even at the squad level, and the raw exigencies of survival tend to send troops scattering to the winds far from the view of comrades, not to mention troop leaders and commanders. Flames and rubble further break up unit cohesion as well as provide defenders with serendipitous tools that multiply the inherent benefits of urban terrain. (*upper right and bottom left*) Garapan, Saipan, 1944 and (*bottom right*) Okinawa, 1945. *Official USMC Photos*

This Marine infantry company command group has paused in the open to coordinate the movement of platoons and squads as well as receive orders from the battalion command post. The Marine farthest to the left is probably an artillery forward observer or naval gunfire coordinator, who must gather data from troops he is supporting, then call and adjust fires on targets he might not be able to see. Lines of command and control are difficult to maintain in urban terrain, and often the reduced vistas lead to the dissemination of bad information that endangers the lives of friendly troops. Even when platoon and squad leaders have access to small radios like the walkie-talkie seen on the far right, conversation can be impeded by loud noises echoing off hard surfaces or by physical barriers. Results can fall short of needs due to misunderstandings caused by noise and visual barriers. Garapan, Saipan, 1944. *Official USMC Photo*

In urban combat, direct-fire weapons, such as this 37mm antitank gun, are extremely useful where walls and doors need to be taken down. Mortars are less reliable unless their fire can be closely observed and minutely controlled. Garapan, Saipan, 1944. *Official USMC Photo*

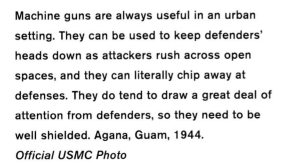

Machine guns are always useful in an urban setting. They can be used to keep defenders' heads down as attackers rush across open spaces, and they can literally chip away at defenses. They do tend to draw a great deal of attention from defenders, so they need to be well shielded. Agana, Guam, 1944.
Official USMC Photo

Cover is what it is in an urban setting. Even a flimsy wall is good cover if a soldier can use it to move without being seen, but in the sort of mixed terrain shown here, it does tend to draw fire. The many nonpenetrating hits shown on this wall exemplify several additional principles of urban combat: enough firepower over a long enough time can drive defenders from good cover; large-caliber hits on one side of a masonry wall can result in casualties on the other side through spalling via kinetic energy that impels materials toward the defenders. Flying debris, even tiny shards, can be as deadly as bullets or shrapnel. Agana, Guam, 1944. *Official USMC Photo*

Rubble is a double-edged sword. Blowing a building apart can cause death or severe injury to defenders as well as flatten city vistas (itself an advantage that cuts two ways), but it also creates hazards for attackers by offering uncountable opportunities for defenders to find cover the human eye cannot discern. There's no good way to cope with rubble in embattled urban settings; it is just another universal factor that attackers and defenders need to adapt to. Tinian, 1944. *Official USMC Photo*

The wary infantryman is the symbol of urban combat. This Marine needs to move, but is it safe? How much looking around can he do before a hidden defender spots him? There are so many possibilities for hunter and hunted that it's often impossible to say which is which. Seoul, Korea, 1950. *Official USMC Photo courtesy of* Leatherneck

In an urban setting, the high ground is typically a tall building, such as this masonry church steeple. It is a perfect spot for a sniper or an artillery forward observer, and it naturally attracts the attention—and fire—of men at ground level. Numerous techniques can be employed to neutralize "high ground," but in the end it requires physical possession to really neutralize it. Then it can be used by your side's snipers and forward observers. Naha, Okinawa, 1945. *Official USMC Photo*

Optimally, large patches of urban terrain can be preliminarily cleared by the swift advance of footborne infantry supported by tanks. Eventually, however, terrain cleared so swiftly must be painstakingly combed on foot, by infantrymen, to locate defenders who have been trapped by the swift advance or intentionally left behind to terrorize rear-echelon troops and headquarters. Seoul, Korea, 1950. *Official USMC Photos courtesy of* Leatherneck

This is what veteran, battle-aware street fighters look like. The nearest Marine walks in a stoop from which he can drop to the ground and return fire in a heartbeat. The Marine directly behind him reflexively checks an opening in his cover even though at least two Marines (the automatic rifleman and the photographer) have already safely passed it. Naha, Okinawa, 1945.
Official USMC Photo

The capture of South Korea's capitol building was cause for an impromptu flag-raising. Hoisting the U.S. national colors at the end of a hard fight is a tradition U.S. Marines adopted in World War II, and it persists to the present day. Seoul, Korea, 1950. *Official USMC Photo courtesy of* Leatherneck

What victorious urban combatants count as a noble victory, residents usually count as the end of an era, the end of life as they knew it. Garapan, Saipan, 1944. *Official USMC Photo*

Chapter 2

GENERAL OFFENSIVE— GENERAL UPRISING

Through 1967, the leaders of the Communist government and armies of the People's Republic of Vietnam—North Vietnam—developed an ambitious and complex plan to force an early victory over the U.S.-supported government of the Republic of Vietnam—South Vietnam. The plan was dubbed "General Offensive–General Uprising." It would involve virtually all North Vietnamese Army (NVA) and Viet Cong (VC) military units arrayed in South Vietnam, including many fresh NVA units dispatched from the North for the purpose.

Battlefield experience in South Vietnam had shown that the powerful American combat forces invariably reacted to a threat against a military force or base with far more vigor and purpose than they did to a threat against a civilian political target, such as a government center or city hall. Communist forces had a powerful bias the other way.

Drawing on Maoist revolutionary doctrine as well as American response patterns, the Communists drew up a plan aimed at pinning American forces to defense of supply routes and out-of-the-way bases (such as Khe Sanh, in the remote northwestern corner of South Vietnam) while the Communists wreaked havoc against South Vietnamese governmental and civilian centers. The entire so-called Tet Offensive of 1968 was aimed at forcing a direct political defeat on the Republic of Vietnam while keeping the politically myopic Americans occupied in defense of far-flung military assets.

Ultimately, if the South Vietnamese people did not in fact rise throughout South Vietnam in support of their northern brothers and sisters, the immense offensive was aimed at wresting South Vietnam's two northernmost provinces, Quang Tri and Thua Thien, into an amalgamation with the North. Thus a key target set aside for special handling was the city of Hue, the former imperial capital of a united Vietnam, now the capital of Thua Thien Province. There is no way to overstate how the capture of Hue by the

Senior General Vo Nguyen Giap commanded all Vietnamese forces that defeated France and established Vietnam as a sovereign nation in the 1950s, after which he stood up the People's Army of Vietnam—the North Vietnamese Army. It was his observation that American combat forces tended to defend military assets over political assets, and this led to the formulation of the Communists' General Offensive-General Uprising of Tet 1968. For all that Giap is adored as the military architect of reunification of a divided Vietnam, the former schoolteacher was a rather plodding tactician who spent seas of his soldiers' blood to learn even the simple lessons new lieutenants are taught at Western service schools. But he did understand the link between military action and political reality, and his mastery of the dichotomy is why he is looked on with such awe. *Colonel Chuck Meadows Collection*

General William Childs Westmoreland, a 1936 West Point graduate, did exceedingly well in World War II as a divisional artillery commander in Europe. He subsequently switched to the infantry and qualified as a paratrooper. He was promoted to major general in 1956 and took command of the 101st Airborne Division in 1958. He next served as superintendent at West Point from 1960 to 1963, then as commanding general of the XVIII Airborne Corps, from which he was sent to Vietnam to command Military Assistance Command, Vietnam. Brainy and militarily shrewd, a haughty and distant officer selected early in his career for high command and nurtured all along the way, Westmoreland fell prey to his political masters, who, in his view, would not allow him to fight his war as a military event. This contravenes Giap's view that Westmoreland *and* his political masters saw and fought the war *only* as a military event denuded of all political considerations. *Colonel Chuck Meadows Collection*

The Republic of Vietnam national colors fly from a military radio tower in southern Hue. *Colonel Chuck Meadows Collection*

Communist armies would undermine the morale and play havoc on the very political psyche of the South.

*

As Communist forces fanned out under cover of an arranged holiday ceasefire to begin their nationwide offensive on the night of January 30–31, 1968, most Army of the Republic of Vietnam (ARVN) units stood down and their troops dispersed to their homes for the year's most important religious and patriotic observance. American units not in hard contact with Communist forces likewise stood down to take a breather from the war, but they remained wary and as fully manned as a liberal year-round leave policy allowed.

By the evening of January 30, virtually all Communist units arrayed to begin the offensive were in place. In the Hue sector, the 4th, 5th, and 6th NVA regiments, each reinforced by numerous combat-hardened VC infantry and

Large parts of the modern southern half of Hue are given over to pleasant tree-lined streets fronted by large homes and mansions, often set apart in walled compounds. From the start of the conflict in the early 1960s and through 1967, Hue was largely untouched by war, a factor that brought a burden of many refugees seeking respite from the war in the countryside and other cities. *Colonel Chuck Meadows Collection*

Once the center of Vietnam's imperial life and long the center of its spiritual life, Hue had been reduced in stature by the French to the role of the political center of Thua Thien Province. Government buildings abounded in the five or six city blocks south of the Perfume River and especially east of National Highway 1. *Colonel Chuck Meadows Collection*

Spreading out from the government areas of the modern southern half of the city were prosperous commercial streets bustling with all manner of trade and commerce, even in the heart of a long war. *Texas Tech Virtual Vietnam Archive/Tommy Carver Collection.*

sapper units, prepared to swamp the symbolic city, which had seen little direct fighting in its environs over the war's many years. In classic siege style, the 5th NVA Regiment was to guard the periphery of the battlefield to keep out

enemy reinforcements. The 4th NVA Regiment, approaching from the south, was to take military and political objectives in the modern part of the city, south of the Perfume River. Among its vital targets was the compound manned by Advisory

Texas Tech Virtual Vietnam Archive/George Jolliff Collection

Team 3 of the U.S. Military Assistance Command, Vietnam (MACV), the so-called MACV Compound. And the 6th NVA Regiment was to seize the older half of the city of Hue, on the northern bank of the Perfume. Its key target was the ancient imperial compound, the Citadel of Hue, as well as the command post of the 1st ARVN Division, in the Citadel's northern corner. In fact, Communist units and political cadres set to operate in Hue had a checklist of 314 separate objectives, from the seizure of the MACV Compound and the 1st ARVN Division command post to the execution of individually named civic leaders, intellectuals, and even schoolteachers.

The southern reaches of the Citadel of Hue with the Dong Ba Market at bottom center and the Nguyen Hoang Bridge just above it. The Imperial Palace occupies the right center area of the photo, directly behind the largest bastion fronting the river. *Official USMC Photo*

The Citadel of Hue, looking almost due north. As with most old fortified cities, homes and businesses encroach on the fortifications, but there is still a good deal of flat, cultivated land to the north and northwest. In this photo, Hue has the look of a pleasant river city dominated by artifacts of its imperial past and as the present abode of a major government center. These it indeed was through the last day of January 1968. *Official USMC Photo*

Through the end of 1967, Hue hosted many American servicemen on in-country leave. The Marines seen here, in October 1967, are approaching the ornate Lin Mu Pagoda, part of the Imperial Palace complex.
Official USMC Photo

This color photo of a wing of the Imperial Palace provides a sense of the degree to which the palace complex was maintained long after the fall of Vietnam's imperium. There are limits to what a poor, war-torn nation in a wet, hot part of the world can spend on such maintenance, but it is apparent that South Vietnam did its very best to protect its heritage.
Colonel Chuck Meadows Collection

This beautiful corner of the Imperial Palace complex was a portion of servant housing. Nevertheless, it is as lovingly maintained as the imperium's ceremonial buildings. *Colonel Chuck Meadows Collection*

Chapter 3

ASSAULT ON HUE

January 30–31, 1968

They came in the night. Covered by a thick, persistent fog, the Communist assault battalions tiptoed out of their secret staging areas all around the city and made their way, as silently as they could, to the lines of departure. In the south, an NVA battalion got a late start over difficult, foggy terrain and thus fell behind schedule. Another battalion bound for southern Hue had been spotted during the night on January 29–30 and was pinned by a two-hour dose of artillery fire that caused it to fall a full day behind schedule.

In the north, inside the Citadel, Brigadier General Ngo Quang Truong, the 1st ARVN Division commander, had had a feeling on January 29 that something was up, so he had put his troops on alert and thrown out patrols. He was acting entirely on intuition, but, sure enough, an ARVN patrol composed of elite reconnaissance troops from the 1st ARVN Division command compound caught sight of a large body of troops on the move and sounded an alarm that ultimately saved the divisional command post from being overrun.

At 0340, ten minutes behind schedule, an NVA rocket battalion set in on hills overlooking western Hue fired a sheaf of 122mm rockets at an area south of the Perfume River and east of National Highway 1. This was the signal for the citywide assault to begin.

The rockets that opened the Tet Offensive in Hue were directed against the MACV Compound, the headquarters of MACV Advisory Team 3, a multiservice, multinational command composed of American soldiers, sailors, Marines, and airmen as well as Australian army advisors. Even before the rockets struck, the compound was rocked by 82mm mortar rounds fired from within a nearby sports stadium.

In the north, a sapper team overwhelmed ARVN guards at the Chanh Tay Gate, near the Citadel's western corner. Immediately, an NVA battalion waiting outside poured into the Citadel and fanned out to seize multiple objectives.

Brigadier General Ngo Quang Truong, the incorruptible commanding general of the 1st ARVN Division, was probably the best general the Army of the Republic of Vietnam ever put in the field. A natural-born fighting general—brave to a fault, cool-headed, and gifted—Truong so impressed the American officers with whom he came in contact that several who were quite senior had him virtually kidnapped aboard an American helicopter when he refused to give up the losing fight as Saigon fell in 1975. On January 29, 1968, Truong intuited that the Communists would break the Tet ceasefire, so he ordered his entire division to stand down from holiday leave while he set up a schedule for active patrolling all around Hue. The patrolling itself delayed several Communist units from getting into assault positions on schedule. *Official U.S. Army Photo courtesy of General Ngo Quang Truong*

The soldiers of the 1st ARVN Division under General Truong's command were smart-looking troops with high morale and excellent fighting skills. Moreover, most of them had been recruited directly from the division's area of operations, so they saw their mission as primarily defending home and family, a force multiplier with profound impact on the division's fighting qualities. *Texas Tech Virtual Vietnam Archive/Douglas Pike Photo Collection*

A direct attack on the interior gate to the 1st ARVN Division command compound was thwarted when the assault team ran into an unexpected barbed-wire barrier. These NVA swiftly improvised an attack that took out four guard bunkers, but the shooting alerted ARVN troops within the compound, and the main assault by most of an NVA battalion was thus

The northern corner of the Citadel of Hue (1) housed the 1st ARVN Division command compound, which remained entirely in ARVN hands despite repeated Communist assaults. Also, note (2) Tay Loc Airfield and (3) the Citadel flagpole. *Texas Tech Virtual Vietnam Archive/Michael J. Morea Collection*

thwarted. A counterattack by thirty ARVN clerks, medics, and even hospital patients collided with a renewed NVA assault and achieved a stalemate. By then, the defenders had formed battle lines and were repelling subsidiary assaults.

An NVA infantry battalion paired with a VC sapper battalion was stymied by an unreconnoitered barbed-wire barrier on the way

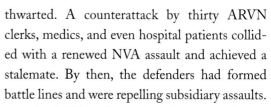

The Citadel of Hue's Tay Loc Airfield, looking west. Communist forces initially seized most of the runway, but the 1st ARVN Ordnance Company fiercely hung on to its depot, the cluster of buildings at the southern end of the runway. Before dawn, however, the defenders were ordered to break contact and make their way to the divisional command post. *Official USMC Photo*

to capture Tay Loc Airfield, in the north-central Citadel. After blundering around in the dark, these units found a way to their objective, but the 1st ARVN Ordnance Company, manning a depot at the airfield, put up fearsome resistance in a toe-to-toe fight that allowed General Truong's elite 250-man Hoc Bao (Black Panther) Company to counterattack.

Well before dawn, the situation within the Citadel had stabilized. ARVN units still held most of Tay Loc Airfield and the entire 1st ARVN Division command compound. Moreover, ARVN reinforcements directly under General Truong's command were on the way in from the periphery of the city.

South of the Perfume, the NVA and VC units that found their way into the city seized all their immediate objectives, save one: the MACV Compound. There, everyone—advisors up to the rank of major, clerks, cooks, drivers, medics, even pilots merely spending the night—turned out for an ad hoc defense that blunted the first onslaught and stood against repeated attempts to breach the walls. An adjacent National Police compound also held out.

Several vital military installations in the southern city were not even molested. These included the compound housing the 1st ARVN Engineer Battalion, the cantonment manned by the headquarters and about half of the 7th ARVN Armored Cavalry Battalion, and the U.S. Navy's Hue LCU Ramp on the southern bank of the Perfume River a few blocks east of Highway 1.

It must be noted that, to the Communist forces, clearing the military opposition was a means to an end. That end was the civil objectives, because of what they symbolized. The Communists were seeking a general uprising. Ultimately, however, passing up or wasting opportunities, or simply failing to destroy military targets, was their undoing.

For all that, despite repeated hit-and-run assaults in the dark by the elite and steadfast thirty-six-man 1st ARVN Reconnaissance

National Highway 1 runs southeast (right) to northwest (left) through the middle of this view. The MACV Compound is above the highway at far right. *Official USMC Photo*

The MACV courtyard with quarters and an office building. Advisors, guards, and administrative personnel defended the compound from the roofs and balconies as well as walls and bunkers around the periphery. Many of the defenders later compared the defense to that at the Alamo. *Texas Tech Virtual Vietnam Archive/Peter Braestrup Collection*

The front gate of the former MACV Compound as seen in 2005. The courtyard and quarters are the same as shown in the previous photo. The facility is now an old soldiers' home. *Courtesy of Colonel Chuck Meadows*

The Republic of Vietnam national colors aloft on the Citadel of Hue's main flagpole. Directly behind is the Imperial Palace grounds. One of the main Communist objectives during the assault phase in Hue was to replace these colors with the banner of the National Liberation Front, South Vietnam's Communist political party. This objective was achieved before dawn on January 31, 1968, the first full day of the Tet Offensive. *Official USMC Photo*

The ARVN's Le Lai Military Camp in southwestern Hue fell into Communist control during the first day of the Tet Offensive. *Official USMC Photo*

Company, an NVA infantry company was able to make its way to the immense flagpole in front of the Citadel overlooking the Perfume River. There, the huge Republic of Vietnam national colors were hauled down and a giant red, yellow, and blue banner—the colors of the National Liberation Front, the Viet Cong—was hoisted in its place. At dawn, when this swap could be seen, the enormity of the Communist gamble could be perceived by one and all. Yet, for all that this was a major political coup, it is not known if it motivated any citizen of Hue to join the Communist cause or take part in a general uprising.

Also in the dark, at about 0500, General Truong streamlined and bolstered his defensive efforts by ordering the 1st ARVN Ordnance Company to abandon its depot at Tay Loc Airfield in favor of reinforcing the 1st ARVN Division command compound. While this move was taking place, Truong contacted headquarters up and down the chain of command, and he was able to piece together a plan to begin the relief of his command compound by ARVN troops alone. After sunup, the 5th NVA Regiment, guarding the periphery to the northwest, stymied relief efforts from that direction, and several companies of the 7th ARVN Armored Cavalry Battalion were virtually annihilated while undertaking three stubborn attacks from the southern outskirts, directly up Highway 1 toward the road bridge that spanned the Perfume River.

The commander of MACV Advisory Team 3 also put out a plea for help from the closest American base, the cantonment and airfield at Phu Bai, on Highway 1, south of the city. There he contacted the command post of Task Force X-Ray, a subheadquarters of the 1st Marine Division. All the army colonel asked his colleagues at Task Force X-Ray to do was send combat troops.

This 7th ARVN Armored Cavalry Battalion M41 light tank was incinerated during the morning of January 31 by Communist troops vying for control of Highway 1 against one of the ARVN unit's three all-out attacks toward MACV and the Nguyen Hoang highway bridge linking the two halves of Hue across the Perfume River.
Official USMC Photo

The Attackers

The North Vietnamese Army and Viet Cong military units that invested most of the city of Hue during the night of January 30–31, 1968, were composed of highly trained elite soldiers considered among the very best their side had in the field. They had painstakingly rehearsed the assault plan on life-size mockups of their objectives and had been sent into battle with assurances of victory not only on the Tet battlefields but also in the war itself. If they suffered from one thing, it was the inability of leaders at all but the highest rank to take responsibility for their actions when their highly polished plans went awry in the face of delays, stubborn or unanticipated resistance, unexpected battlefield conditions, or unanticipated barriers. This shortfall in initiative contributed mightily to the ability of ARVN troops and MACV Advisory Team 3 to hold out through the first night of the battle for Hue.

Texas Tech Virtual Vietnam Archive

Texas Tech Virtual Vietnam Archive/Donald Jellema Collection

Chapter 4

SEND IN THE MARINES

January 31, 1968

The first U.S. Marine tactical unit to be alerted for a mission to Hue was Captain Gordon Batcheller's Alpha Company, 1st Battalion, 1st Marine Regiment (Alpha/1/1).

It is something of a stretch to think of Alpha/1/1 as a "tactical unit" per se. Two combat-diminished platoons and the company field headquarters happened to be overnighting in the sprawling Marine base at Phu Bai, about 17 kilometers south of Hue on National Highway 1, because the 1st Battalion, 1st Marines, was displacing southward following a month of duty along the Demilitarized Zone (DMZ) between North Vietnam and South Vietnam. The company had been the last element of 1/1 to leave the DMZ, and it had gotten split up on January 30 when there weren't enough trucks to move the entire unit before nightfall. Also making it to Phu Bai late on January 30 was the 1/1 forward command element under Lieutenant Colonel Marcus Gravel.

At dawn on January 31, Captain Batcheller received a sketchy briefing before being ordered to move his truncated company out of Phu Bai under escort from two U.S. Army M55 trucks equipped with quadruple .50-caliber machine-gun mounts to conduct a vaguely defined mission toward the coast. After setting out, Alpha/1/1 was ordered to turn north on Highway 1 to relieve the MACV Advisory Team 3 compound in Hue. Task Force X-Ray, which issued the order from its Phu Bai command post, had no details to offer.

The fog-shrouded two-lane highway was deserted, something the troops took as a bad sign. But the ride was trouble-free all the way to a bridged creek about 3 kilometers south of MACV. Here, the small truck serial carrying Alpha/1/1 slowed precipitously to avoid running into the rear of five Marine M48 tanks that had stopped on the foggy roadway. Captain Batcheller dismounted to speak to the Marine major who was leading what turned out to be a platoon of Alpha Company, 3d Tank Battalion, which was on its way to the Hue LCU Ramp for a lift north. The major showed Batcheller where a severely

Captain Gordon Batcheller, the commander of Alpha Company, 1/1, was severely wounded on January 31, 1968, on the southern approaches to Hue. He was evacuated under fire and trucked to Phu Bai. *Courtesy of Colonel Gordon Batcheller*

A Marine Corps M48 main battle tank, the type encountered on National Highway 1 by Alpha Company, 1/1, on January 31. The five 3d Tank Battalion M48s were to have been transferred by landing craft from the Hue LCU Ramp to Quang Tri Province as part of the 3d Marine Division's move, but they ended up staying in Hue for the entire battle. *Official USMC Photo*

Lieutenant Colonel Mark Gravel, the commanding officer of the 1st Battalion, 1st Marines. Gravel sports the rank insignia of an ARVN lieutenant colonel on his helmet.
Courtesy of the late Colonel Marcus Gravel

damaged ARVN M41 light tank sat just beside the roadway. The charred corpse of an ARVN tanker hung gruesomely from a turret hatch. All five M48s had unlimbered their guns, and crewmen busily scanned the terrain ahead. The arrival of several truckloads of infantry gave the wary tankers confidence to move once again toward Hue.

A few hundred yards beyond the creek the ad hoc tank-infantry team ran into buildings occupied by troops whose uniforms could not be seen clearly. Batcheller ordered his two officer-less infantry platoons to jump down from the trucks to clear buildings on both sides of the highway. The troops hunkered down ahead turned out to be ARVNs, but NVA soldiers hiding out nearby opened fire, and several Alpha/1/1 Marines were injured in a brief firefight. The wounded were loaded aboard a truck and dispatched to Phu Bai, and the rest of the combat force drove forward toward Hue.

Golf/2/5 Marines aboard a truck at Phu Bai moments before setting out on the company's blind mission to Hue. *Courtesy of Dr. Jerome Nadolski*

This U.S. Army M42 Duster joined the Golf/2/5 convoy as it left Phu Bai bound for Hue. *Courtesy of Douglas Blayney*

About 700 meters north of the creek, Highway 1 took a sharp right turn to due north and entered a built-up area in which at least a long block of two-story buildings dominated the roadway. The confined roadway then debouched onto the short An Cuu Bridge across the Phu Cam Canal, the true southern extremity of the Hue municipality. As Batcheller and the tank major talked about an advance to and then beyond the traffic circle, a convoy of 3d Marine Division work vehicles on its way to the Hue LCU Ramp arrived from the rear. The Marine lieutenant colonel in charge jumped down to converse with Batcheller and the major.

The decision was made to move into the confined area at a robust speed, all guns blazing. This drew automatic weapons and RPG fire from several directions. The senior Alpha Company hospital corpsman and a radioman were killed and other Marines were wounded, but the lengthening convoy ran the gauntlet, crossed the undefended An Cuu Bridge, and hurtled forward through another narrow 600-meter-long corridor of buildings to the broad expanse of a traffic circle fronting a wide kilometer-long canefield that had to be traversed via a long two-lane causeway. About halfway up the causeway was a compound that appeared to be manned by friendly troops.

Captain Chuck Meadows was on his second tour as an infantry company commander when his Golf/2/5 was called out to "rescue" the 1st ARVN Division command post from Communist forces that threatened to overwhelm it on the first morning of the Tet Offensive. *Courtesy of Colonel Chuck Meadows*

At least six ARVN M41 tanks and an armored personnel carrier were arrayed around the traffic circle. It was grim; they were all wrecked and devoid of a living soul.

All the vehicles and troops dispersed while the tanks engaged hostile targets and the commanders discussed options. Captain Batcheller also raised his battalion's forward command group

The Golf/2/5 convoy enters a built-up area immediately south of the Phu Cam Canal. *Courtesy of Dr. Jerome Nadolski*

Marine truck drivers hunker down and attempt to spot targets as their convoy is taken under fire on the southern outskirts of Hue, near the big traffic circle. *Courtesy of Dr. Jerome Nadolski*

and spoke with Lieutenant Colonel Gravel. It turned out that Gravel and his command team were on the way up Highway 1 from Phu Bai.

Under covering fire from the M55 quad-.50 trucks, the convoy headed onto the open causeway. In short order it was swept by fire. Captain Batcheller was among those hit; he tumbled into a tangle of barbed wire. Command of Alpha/1/1 passed to Gunnery Sergeant J. L. Canley, who maneuvered his troops and all five tanks ahead with a vengeance. Soon, as Lieutenant Colonel Gravel

arrived near the traffic circle, the main body of Alpha/1/1 and the tanks disappeared into the cityscape on the far side of the causeway, engrossed in a deliberate advance to reach, and thus relieve, the MACV warriors a few blocks ahead.

As Gravel got to work organizing the recovery and care of the Alpha/1/1 wounded, a 160-man Marine infantry company—Captain Chuck Meadows' Golf Company, 2d Battalion, 5th Marines (Golf/2/5)—hurtled across the An Cuu Bridge and roared to a halt near the traffic

Golf/2/5 Marines scan the gas station fronting on the traffic circle. The spire of Hue Cathedral is visible at far right, which indicates that the Marines are looking west. *Courtesy of Dr. Jerome Nadolski*

Captain Chuck Meadows took temporary cover in this gas station when his company was first fired on in southern Hue. He managed to locate a Hue street map in the office and used it throughout the battle. For a time, it was the only map his battalion had of the battlefield. This photo was taken in 2005. *Courtesy of Colonel Chuck Meadows*

Marines from Golf/2/5 stand to in the MACV Compound courtyard during the short interval between their arrival and shoving off to bolster the 1st ARVN Division command post in the Citadel of Hue. *Courtesy of Douglas Blayney*

As a Vietnamese movie cameraman moves to a safer spot in Doc Lao Park, two MACV personnel—a Marine (right) and a soldier—prepare to cover Golf/2/5's advance across the Perfume River. *Texas Tech Virtual Vietnam Archive*

circle. Golf/2/5 had been the only Marine infantry company formally assigned to Phu Bai on January 30, and it had spent the night in the field as a breakwater against possible attacks. It had gotten back into the base at about the time Alpha/1/1 left. The company was "chopped" to the control of 1/1, Meadows and Gravel shook hands, Gravel left to take the 1/1 forward command element north, and Golf/2/5 was rushed aboard trucks and sent north with a pair of army tracked M42 dual-40mm gun carriers, known as Dusters. Meadows' mission—and Gravel's—was to bypass MACV, advance across the Perfume River, and reinforce the embattled 1st ARVN Division Command compound in the northern corner of the Citadel of Hue.

The Golf/2/5 convoy was nosing onto the causeway before anyone noticed the Alpha/1/1 wounded or Gravel's headquarters vehicles. But Meadows' troops had seen the wrecked M41 at the creek and the others arrayed around the traffic circle. The picture suddenly became absolutely clear as small-arms fire struck the convoy from the left. All the way at the far eastern edge of the canefield,

Marines from the Golf/2/5 platoon left behind on the southern bank covered the crossing from Doc Lao Park with intense fire from M16 assault rifles and M60 medium machine guns.
Official USMC Photo

clumps of khaki-clad infantrymen plodded northward. They were a late-arriving NVA battalion. Then the Alpha/1/1 casualties came into focus. An NVA machine gun finally caused all the new arrivals to abandon the trucks, seek cover, and return fire. Captain Meadows took cover in a gas station, where he unearthed the first Hue city map to arrive in the hands of the relief troops.

With that, once the Marines realized that the NVA battalion on the far left was more interested in making its way into the city than engaging in a long-range firefight with a Marine infantry company, Golf/2/5 saddled up and took off across the causeway, leaving Gravel to deal with the Alpha/1/1 wounded.

The advance of Alpha/1/1 and the Marine tanks was still progressing under weak enemy fire along Highway 1, but the lead infantry elements led the 3d Marine Division work convoy into the MACV courtyard without much trouble, and Golf/2/5 arrived with its Duster escort without a problem. To the MACV warriors manning the barricades, the new faces and vast increase in power meant the world. Shortly, as Alpha/1/1 took over key defensive positions, trucks manned by MACV volunteers headed out to evacuate the Alpha/1/1 casualties, either south to Phu Bai or north to MACV.

This aerial photo shows Golf/2/5's route from midway across the Nguyen Hoang Bridge to the street leading to the Citadel's Thuong Tu Gate. It's a very long walk through enemy-held cityscape.
Official USMC Photo

In due course, Lieutenant Colonel Gravel reported in with news for the MACV commander that he and Golf/2/5 were under orders to cross the nearby Nguyen Hoang Bridge spanning the Perfume River, and then advance to the 1st ARVN Division command compound. The MACV commander was incredulous, and so was Gravel, after the tactical situation was made clear to him. He and the army colonel petitioned Task Force X-Ray for a reprieve, but the Marine brigadier general in command was adamant.

At 1610, following a rest and armed with some grim advice from the MACV colonel, Golf/2/5 and the 1/1 forward command element loaded onto trucks and advanced a block to the bridge approach. Some Alpha/1/1 Marines and assorted MACV warriors up to the rank of major had turned out on the river edge of Doc Lao Park to offer supporting fire. Captain Meadows decided to leave one of his platoons behind to provide the crossing with even more fire support.

The main body of Golf/2/5 was covered to the halfway point by the steeply arching roadway, but as soon as the first troops peered over the bridge horizon, an NVA heavy machine gun opened fire from a bunker at the northern foot of the span.

As Marines and soldiers in Doc Lao Park opened fire, two Marine CH-46 troop helicopters on a medevac run to MACV swooped off to avoid the melee. A pair of U.S. Navy riverine patrol boats (PBRs) based at the Hue LCU Ramp sallied into the river and opened fire at NVA machine guns. As fire superiority tipped toward the Americans, the CH-46s landed in the park to take casualties aboard. But Golf/2/5 was still under fire on the narrow roadway over the river. An M60 team leader was killed by the NVA .51-caliber machine gun as he got his gun into action, but Corporal Lester Tully surged forward and grenaded the bunker, in which five NVA were killed.

The main body of Golf/2/5 advanced to the northern bank and regrouped. As it did,

Lieutenant Colonel Gravel arrived with several trucks and his command group. The headquarters troops gathered the Golf/2/5 casualties as the truck drivers fired .50-caliber machine guns at surrounding buildings.

Free of its casualties, Golf/2/5 moved out to the left to follow Highway 1 beneath the Citadel wall a long block to the side street that ran two more blocks through the Thuong Tu Gate, and then another kilometer through crowded cityscape to the nearest entrance to the 1st ARVN Division command compound. No one there believed the company would get anywhere near its objective.

The walk from the bridge to the Thuong Tu Gate was almost uneventful; the lead squad

The intersection of Highway 1 and the Thuong Tu Gate road, looking toward the Citadel. Courtesy of Colonel Chuck Meadows

This view is just inside the Thuong Tu Gate road from the corner of Highway 1, as it appeared in 2005. The gate is visible at left center, at the end of a bridge across a moat. Courtesy of Colonel Chuck Meadows

Captain Chuck Meadows advanced to the near tree to monitor the fight on the Thuong Tu Gate road and became pinned there by intense fire. He eventually set down his M16 and advanced about 50 yards down the road to rescue a fallen Golf/2/5 Marine. This photo was taken in 2005. *Courtesy of Colonel Chuck Meadows*

Golf/2/5 survivors of the ill-advised river crossing toward the 1st ARVN Division command compound upon their return to the MACV Compound late on January 31, 1968. At far right, showing off a captured M1 carbine, is Corporal Lester Tully, who single-handedly silenced an NVA machine-gun bunker at the northern foot of the Nguyen Hoang Bridge. *Courtesy of Douglas Blayney*

leader was lightly wounded in an exchange with a sniper. The Golf/2/5 Marines had never fought in a city, but most of them had achieved a postdoctoral level of combat savvy. They knew how to move. Nevertheless, the lead squad was nailed by heavy fire as soon as it turned the corner into the gate road. As many as ten Marines were bowled off their feet, and everyone else scrambled for cover.

The fire was coming from up the street *and* outside the intersection, toward the river or farther along Highway 1. It had the lead squad pinned in the street and along the sidewalk, and there was no safe way to push troops forward. Captain Meadows dashed forward to the cover of a tree just around the corner, toward the Thuong Tu Gate. He was stuck there, barely able to avoid injury.

It took everything Golf/2/5 had to extricate the main body of the lead platoon from the crossfire. Nevertheless, the company commander remained trapped behind his tree, and several others were also pinned. In the open were two wounded Marines and a wounded corpsman. A flatbed truck was hot-wired and sent up the street as a moving shield. Two Marines accompanying the truck pulled the wounded corpsman in, but he had already bled to death. And two trapped Marines who were now able to move pulled the other wounded Marine, the previously wounded squad leader, to safety. But the last wounded Marine still lay in the open. Captain Meadows dumped his M16 and rushed 50 yards into the open to grab the inert man by the belt and heave him back. They were halfway to safety when a radioman rushed from cover to assist. The Marine was pulled in, but he was dead when he got there.

In all, the 160-man infantry company had sustained 5 killed and 44 wounded since leaving Phu Bai—losses of 35 percent to an already understrength unit. Chuck Meadows had had enough. He told Mark Gravel he had had enough. Gravel, whose battalion operations officer had just been killed by a loose grenade while loading Golf Company casualties beside the bridge, had had enough too. He called off the ill-conceived mission to the Citadel and ordered everyone back to MACV. Following a tricky withdrawal across the bridge, dead, wounded, and living all were inside the compound by 1900 hours.

Gravel took several tanks and a handful of volunteers out in the late afternoon on an unsuccessful bid to rescue several Americans living in the city. Scores of Vietnamese refugees joined him on the uneventful trip back to MACV. That evening, a rather daring helicopter rescue was laid on at Doc Lao Park to clear all the wounded out of the otherwise overwhelmed MACV medical dispensary.

That night, Gravel had time to consider his own knowledge of urban combat. It wasn't much, but he knew he needed more troops to do more than guard the MACV "Alamo." One point he came up with was that using streets as axes of advance was suicidal. In this, he came to the same conclusion reached by Marines confronted with cityscapes in the Pacific and Korea: wherever possible, advance along interior pathways created by blowing holes in walls between buildings. That was as far as he got with a plan that night, but it was a good start.

A point Gravel failed to perceive was that the arrival of two Marine infantry companies and five tanks at MACV had turned the guiding concepts of urban warfare on their heads. The MACV enclave was effectively a lodgment *within* an urban combat zone. Instead of having to start at the outside and grind toward the center, they were already well inside. They could grind outward from MACV while a classic siege ring was thrown up outside the city to impinge on NVA and VC access to or egress from the city. Brigadier General Ngo Quang Truong's 1st ARVN Division command compound was the same kind of lodgment, and it offered the same kind of possibilities.

*

The first aerial medevac flights out of Hue were made aboard CH-46 medium helicopters that dashed into an improvised helipad in Doc Lao Park on the afternoon of January 31. *Official USMC Photo*

After only a few minutes in the air, casualties from Hue were unloaded alongside the medical-surgical facility at Phu Bai. A CH-46 is overhead the Quonset hut housing a portion of the medical facility.

Chapter 5

STABILIZING
THE LODGMENT

February 1–2, 1968

During the night of January 31–February 1, the two operational headquarters with overlapping responsibility for the Hue tactical area—the III Marine Amphibious Force (III MAF) and the I ARVN Corps—agreed to split the Hue battlefield at the northern bank of the Perfume River barrier separating the two halves of the city. The 1st ARVN Division would retain control north of the river and Task Force X-Ray would control the battle on and south of the river.

During the morning of February 1, Task Force X-Ray ordered the 1st Marine Regiment (1st Marines) to assume tactical control over combat units in the southern city—that is, two battered Marine infantry companies and the 1/1 forward command element. The 1st Marines dubbed the mission Operation Hue City and assigned 1/1 "the mission of conducting sweep and clear operations in [the] assigned area of operations to destroy enemy forces, protect U.S. nationals, and restore [the southern portion] of the city to U.S. control."

Communist forces in southern Hue used February 1 to consolidate and dig in. For the most part, in allegiance to a plan that was already badly out of date, they dug in at the periphery, as if Hue were going to be assaulted in the classic manner of sieges, from the outside in.

The only real objective the Communists had not overcome in southern Hue was the Thua Thien Provincial Prison. Unfortunately, pleas for help from the prison's defenders caused Task Force X-Ray to focus an abundance of attention on relieving the place with the two ragged infantry companies hunkered down at the MACV Compound. Lieutenant Colonel Mark Gravel, who realized only too clearly how powerless his two-company battalion was to effect any such relief mission, did his best to ignore requests to move on the prison. The prison was 1,200 meters from MACV, and it was all cityscape in between. Near the prison was the Thua Thien Province Administration

This Alpha/1/1 Marine displays two holes in his helmet, the only result of a February 1 run-in with an NVA sniper near the MACV Compound. *Official USMC Photo by Sergeant William L. Dickman*

The February 1–2 battlefield, showing the MACV Compound, an ARVN military camp, the Hue University main compound, the Highway 1 traffic circle, Doc Lao Park, and the Hue LCU Ramp. *Official USMC Photo*

The 2d Battalion, 5th Marines, was a savvy, powerful force to be reckoned with when it engaged Communist troops in the bush. This 2/5 squad is laying down suppressive fire so another unit can cross open ground. City fighting was something else. Until members of 2/5 reached Hue, they had no experience—and no training—to prepare them for urban combat. *Official USMC Photo by Gunnery Sergeant C. Lane*

The Fox/2/5 commanding officer in Hue was twenty-eight-year-old Captain Mike Downs, who had the distinction of being married to the younger daughter of Marine Corps legend Lieutenant General Lewis B. "Chesty" Puller. Downs was considered a smart, gutsy commander and a fearless combat leader. *Courtesy of Brigadier General Mike Downs*

Center, where a tall flagpole showed the National Liberation Front colors. And around the administration complex, which Task Force X-Ray also wanted Gravel to seize, were a public health complex, a treasury building, the municipal power station, and other structures, facilities, and compounds the Communist political masters were not going to leave without a huge fight. Gravel grasped the impossibility of the mission, but Task Force X-Ray carped about it all day.

A platoon of Golf/2/5, the Golf/2/5 command group, a handful of MACV volunteers, and two M48 tanks jumped off toward the prison at 0700, February 1. These troops were unable to fight across Highway 1 until several hours of intense battle had passed. Once across Highway 1, the tiny combat force tried to fight its way

Elements of Fox/2/5 assemble around an ARVN M41 light tank shortly after landing in Doc Lao Park. Mistakenly assuming they were going to Hue for a quick job, the troops all left their packs on a battlefield south of Phu Bai. *Courtesy of Alexander Kandic*

A Fox/2/5 Marine armed with an M14 rifle takes aim at a target on the northern bank of the Perfume River. *Courtesy of Alexander Kandic*

down Tran Cao Van Street. It bullied ahead all of 15 meters and eventually gave up the effort more than six long blocks short of the objective.

While one platoon of Golf/2/5 was blocked in its bid for the prison, another advanced south on Highway 1 to rescue U.S. State Department officials from their homes near the canefield. Two of the officials were brought safely to MACV.

Golf/2/5's remaining platoon was dispatched to Phu Bai as convoy escort when Task Force X-Ray requested that all the trucks that had carried Marines to Hue on January 31 be returned. The two M55 quad-.50 trucks went out with the convoy. This left Mark Gravel with two infantry companies, each short an infantry platoon, two M42 Dusters, and five M48 tanks. The convoy reached Phu Bai with only minor resistance, and the Golf/2/5 platoon commander delivered a message that went a long way toward straightening out the viewpoints of senior commanders attempting to fight a battle blind and by remote control.

*

More than a full day before Task Force X-Ray achieved new insights, Captain Mike Downs' Fox Company, 2/5, was literally snatched

from a hot battlefield 8 kilometers south of Phu Bai and given orders to join the fight in Hue. Fox/2/5 had reached Phu Bai aboard trucks at noon on January 31, and Captain Downs was given a sketchy briefing. The troops ate hot chow for supper and slept in tents that night. Two 106mm recoilless rifles and two 81mm mortars were attached to the company, and all hands

This aerial view beautifully illustrates the Hue University compound, the Highway 1 traffic circle, and the approach to the Nguyen Hoang Bridge. *Official USMC Photo*

Le Loi Street bordering Doc Lao Park and looking southwest toward the traffic circle on the southern approach to the Nguyen Hoang Bridge. *Courtesy of Douglas Blayney*

drew ammunition. Then all but several squads for whom there was no room lifted out of Phu Bai at about 1500 aboard CH-46 helicopters that also were loaded with as much ammunition as could be squeezed aboard.

Fox/2/5's helos set down in Doc Lao Park as NVA and VC gunners nearby tried to shoot them down. The Fox/2/5 veterans poured off the

CH-46s as if the park was their first combat objective. The helos returned to Phu Bai to pick up the remaining troops and more munitions.

As soon as two Fox/2/5 platoons had assembled at MACV, Lieutenant Colonel Gravel ordered Captain Downs to relieve the battered Golf/2/5 platoon on Tran Cao Van Street and then fight on toward the provincial prison. Guided by a U.S. Air Force sergeant who lived in town, the main body of Fox/2/5 joined with the two M48s that had been assigned to Golf/2/5's luckless platoon. Captain Chuck Meadows turned the battlefield over to Downs and withdrew with his troops. Then one Fox/2/5 platoon turned the corner from Highway 1. The NVA were well entrenched, with terrific fields of fire from upper stories. Marines at ground level couldn't even see them. The Fox/2/5 platoon was hammered. The advance quickly stalled; there were dead and wounded everywhere. It was all the platoon could do to pull back, and that process was painfully slow and yet more costly. In the end, Golf/2/5 lost two killed and five wounded on

The traffic circle looking northwest up Highway 1 toward the Nguyen Hoang Bridge. The wreckage at right is a 7th ARVN Armored Cavalry Battalion armored personnel carrier destroyed in that unit's vain bid to clear Highway 1 on January 31. The Marines in the photo are closing in to secure the circle and all four corners of the large intersection of Highway 1 and Le Loi Street. *Official USMC Photo by First Lieutenant P. T. Cummins*

The traffic circle changed hands among Marine units several times between January 31 and February 3 and was not always under direct Marine or MACV control. As the plan to take Hue's government center evolved over that period, Le Loi Street running southwest from the circle was to become a key axis of advance and supply route. To the northeast, Le Loi bordered Doc Lao Park and, indeed, was the only access to the U.S. Navy's Hue LCU Ramp. It also dominated the approach to the Nguyen Hoang Bridge and could be defended to block a Communist attack or reinforcement efforts from the northern bank of the Perfume River. *Official USMC Photos*

Downs and Gravel agreed to a plan of action, but Downs asked leave to put his views in writing to Task Force X-Ray. Gravel agreed. With the help of the tank major who had reached MACV with Alpha/1/1, Downs wrote a powerfully logical message that earned his company a reprieve. Still later, however, Task Force X-Ray ordered Gravel to mount an all-out daylight assault toward the prison. Gravel knew he didn't have enough troops or supporting arms, but he had no choice but to draw up a plan. In the end, this plan dictated the course of the battle in southern Hue.

Late in the afternoon of February 1, two companies and the forward headquarters of 2/5 were still in the fight south of Phu Bai when

During a Fox/2/5 stint at the traffic circle, two young Vietnamese girls, no doubt refugees, appeared in the midst of the armed Marines from the direction of the Nguyen Hoang Bridge. *Courtesy of Alexander Kandic*

Tran Cao Van Street, and Fox/2/5 lost four dead and eleven wounded.

Late that night, Captain Downs was ordered to make for the Provincial Prison under cover of darkness. He had no real information about the prison, so when Mark Gravel pointed to it on a map and said that the night attack had been ordered by Task Force X-Ray, the voluble company commander became volubly perturbed.

Task Force X-Ray ordered the command group and one company to disengage and report for orders. The battalion commander, Lieutenant Colonel Ernie Cheatham, decided to leave Echo/2/5 behind and report with Captain George R. "Ron" Christmas's Hotel/2/5. When they arrived, Christmas was ordered to leave for Hue via truck convoy on February 2, but Cheatham was given no mission.

*

February 2 was a day of consolidation in the tiny American enclave in southern Hue. A Golf/2/5 infantry platoon on its way to rescue American serviceman manning a radio facility was hit on Highway 1 south of MACV, but it fought through and brought in the refugees during the afternoon.

At noon, the rest of Golf/2/5 was ordered to cross Highway 1 and fight its way into the main campus of Hue University. This was the first step in the Operation Hue City plan to reach the provincial prison—a block-by-block advance southwest from Highway 1. The advance was strongly opposed by infantry supported by .51-caliber heavy machine guns and recoilless rifles, but the two 81mm mortars brought in by Fox/2/5 a day earlier were used to excellent effect even though that use was in defiance of a I ARVN Corps directive that no supporting arms be used in the city. The Golf/2/5 Marines entered the three-story structure at 1445 and set to clearing it, room by room.

*

Fox/2/5 spent the morning of February 2 securing the perimeter around MACV. The task required the clearance of several buildings and compounds belonging to the national, provincial, or municipal governments that either butted up against MACV or barred the way to Doc Lao Park and the Hue LCU Ramp. Among these objectives was the Hue Directorate of Police, whose armory was best retained in friendly hands.

Elements of Alpha/1/1 held on to the park and helped to expand the perimeter right around MACV. After a large part of the main Hue University compound had fallen to Golf/2/5 it was turned over to Alpha/1/1, which went on clearing the immense building, room by room.

Throughout the morning, the 1st Marines command post in Phu Bai helped Hotel/2/5 to organize a road convoy that eventually incorporated Alpha/1/1 stragglers and reinforcements for the Marine infantry companies engaged in Hue. The two army M55 quad-.50 trucks, two more M42 Dusters, and a pair of M50 Ontos recoilless rifle carriers were also mustered for the run to Hue. The troops carried as much ammunition as they could, and all the trucks were crammed full with it. It took until 1417 for the convoy to head out; delays were caused by late additions and bad weather.

Working on advice from the Golf/2/5 platoon commander, Captain Ron Christmas

Captain Ron Christmas, who commanded Hotel/2/5, was held in the highest regard by his troops and his superiors. The "M16" shown in this battlefield photo is a toy. *Official USMC Photo by Sergeant William L. Dickman*

A 2/5, 106mm recoilless rifle attached to Hotel/2/5 is set up, aimed, and fired directly into the oblique northern corner of Hue University. The weapon appears to be set in just in front of the traffic circle. Note the immense backblast created when the 106 is fired. *Official USMC Photos by Sergeant William L. Dickman*

formulated a simple plan for traversing hostile country between Phu Bai and MACV: advance at best speed and don't stop for anything. And that the convoy did, until the main body hurtled off the canefield causeway only blocks from MACV. Here the NVA sprang an ambush and prematurely detonated an explosive device in the middle of the roadway. The lead truck drove into the smoke-shrouded crater, and everything came to a standstill. One of the Dusters and truckloads of infantrymen on foot advanced to engage the NVA shooters while the dazed Marines manning the lead truck sorted themselves out. An artillery forward observer assigned to Hotel/2/5 was trapped beneath the front bumper of the lead truck; there was no getting him out. As soon as the NVA had been overcome—killed or dispersed—Captain Christmas got the troops back aboard the trucks and ordered the convoy to dash to MACV. He was unaware that he left behind a disabled officer and three lightly wounded Alpha/1/1 corporals who were looking out for him. The convoy reached MACV without further ado, and the three corporals fought their way to MACV on foot after the officer succumbed to his

injuries. His body was recovered as soon as Christmas found out what had happened.

When Hotel/2/5 had sorted itself out at MACV, it was sent across Highway 1 to relieve Alpha/1/1, which had nearly finished clearing the University compound. All the Alpha/1/1 new arrivals and several replacements joined the company when the main body returned to MACV. Among the new arrivals were two second lieutenants. The senior of the two, 2d Lieutenant Ray Smith, assumed command from Gunnery Sergeant J. L. Canley. Shortly, Lieutenant Smith's

revivified company crossed Le Loi Street and occupied several public buildings in the southwestern corner of Doc Lao Park.

While the bulk of Hotel/2/5 scoured Hue University for NVA and VC stragglers, the company's three 60mm mortars were set up in the

courtyard, and soon they were firing at suspected Communist strongholds to the northwest.

A large NVA force bolstered by supporting arms attacked Alpha/1/1 and Hotel/2/5 at 1815. Sheets of small-arms fire were traded, and one of the five precious M48 tanks was disabled by a 75mm recoilless rifle round. The Marines gained fire superiority in due course, and the battle subsided at 2200. One Marine was killed in this fight, and eight were wounded.

*

Unbelievably, in the early evening, Fox/2/5 received another order from Task Force X-Ray to attack the Thua Thien Provincial Prison. Captain Downs was given no recourse, so he deployed two of his platoons in column and stepped off down Truong Dinh Street to begin the advance adjacent to the long southeastern wall of Hue University. The lead squad made it as far as the intersection with Ly Thuong Kiet Street, but no farther. The lead squad leader, who was on point, was shot dead in a brief exchange with an NVA rifleman, and then an accompanying tank was grazed by a rocket-propelled grenade (RPG). Two Marines were wounded in an effort to retrieve the dead sergeant, and then two other Marines brought him in following a desperate personal battle in

Second Lieutenant Ray Smith, the senior of Alpha/1/1's only two officers, assumed command of the company upon his arrival in Hue on the afternoon of February 2. Smith, who ultimately pinned on two stars, was one of four Operation Hue City unit commanders to attain flag rank. *Courtesy of the late Colonel Marcus Gravel*

which one fired two M16s at once while the other dragged the dead man to cover. As soon as gunfire and M79 grenades had overcome the enemy fire, Downs called off the attack once and for all. In all on February 2, Fox/2/5 lost one Marine killed and sixteen wounded.

That night, a turncoat led NVA and VC troops to victory over the Provincial Prison's stalwart defenders. Many of the 2,200 inmates, mainly political prisoners, joined the VC, while criminals of various stripes were turned loose to sow fear and dismay throughout the beleaguered city.

On the second and third days of fighting in Hue, the Marine force operating under the command of Lieutenant Colonel Mark Gravel had more than doubled in size. It had secured MACV and its immediate environs, had an ad hoc helipad in firm control at Doc Lao Park, had access to the sea via the Hue LCU Ramp, and had begun building a foundation from which an attack toward the important political objectives southwest of Highway 1 could be mounted. Given the realities of urban combat, casualties had been held to a minimum, and the troops were getting better and better as they improvised the alien but necessary methods it would take to achieve victory.

A severely wounded Alpha/1/1 Marine is lowered gingerly from the roof of the Hue University compound on the afternoon of February 2. *Official USMC Photo by Sergeant William L. Dickman*

Chapter 6

THE
SIX-BLOCK WAR

February 3–6, 1968

February 3

Throughout the morning of February 3, the fighting northeast of Highway 1 mostly involved nickel-and-dime killings. At sunup, one NVA soldier was shot dead as he tried to maneuver a satchel charge toward a building on the northeastern side of the MACV Compound. At 0800, Hotel/2/5 Marines manning an upper-story window in Hue University spotted a squad of NVA in the street below. The Marines fired their weapons and four 40mm M72 LAAW rockets (light antitank assault weapon). They claimed six NVA killed. At 0900, the commander of one of the M48 tanks saw three NVA soldiers dart into the open, and he killed all three with thirty rounds from his .50-caliber cupola machine gun. And so it went.

The big news of February 3 was that the 1st Marines forward command post and the 2/5 command group had been ordered to Hue from Phu Bai. No one in the world was happier to hear that news than Lieutenant Colonel Mark Gravel.

*

During the time between his arrival in Phu Bai on February 2 and his scheduled February 3 departure, Lieutenant Colonel Ernie Cheatham, the 2/5 commander, tried to learn as much as he could about fighting in a built-up area. Cheatham realized with a considerable jolt that he had never been trained to fight in a built-up area, and, in his former job as the 5th Marines operations officer, he had never sent other Marines to fight in a built-up area. Cheatham's battalion would certainly be called upon to clear terrain measured in square yards, but it would also have to fight in three dimensions—the height of buildings as well as their lengths and breadths. Hard work on his memory produced a vague recollection of viewing a British army training film in 1953 in which the Brits did a lot of yelling, lobbed grenades into rooms, and fired their weapons for all they were worth as they stepped into the rooms they had just grenaded.

Somewhere in the 5th Marines regimental command post, Cheatham knew, were several

On the morning of February 3, 1968, a platoon of Alpha/1/1 is rousted from a rest in Doc Lao Park and ordered to secure still more ground around MACV. *Official USMC Photo*

Lieutenant Colonel Ernie Cheatham, the beloved commanding officer of 2/5, had been a Marine since 1952, except to play professional football during the 1954–1955 season. He was all the things superiors and subordinates wanted in a Marine officer—brave, smart, hardworking, firm, and kind. *Courtesy of Lieutenant General Ernest C. Cheatham Jr.*

footlockers filled with field manuals on tactics. He found the cache and quickly reviewed the slim haul of materials devoted to combat in urban terrain—manuals titled *Combat in Built-up Areas* and *Attack on a Fortified Position*. What it all boiled down to was that the best way to fight through a city was to gas the enemy, blow things up, and then comb the ruins.

Armed with this information, Cheatham ordered his battalion's 106mm Recoilless Rifle Platoon to ready the remaining six of its weapons—two had been flown to Hue with Fox/2/5—and as much ammunition as the gun-

An Alpha/1/1 rifleman advances near MACV under cover of one of the two Marine 106mm recoilless rifles in Hue on the morning of February 3. *Official USMC Photo by Sergeant Bruce Atwell*

ners could beg, borrow, or steal. Next, Cheatham sent his armorers out to scrounge every loose tear-gas grenade and gas mask they could find in Phu Bai. He also ordered them to stock up on plastique explosives, every M79 grenade and hand grenade they could locate, and even obsolescent rifle grenades. Speaking of obsolescent weapons, Cheatham decided to unearth the battalion's flamethrowers and, more important, its 3.5-inch rocket launchers—Korean War–vintage bazookas—which recently had been turned in for LAAWs. Cheatham knew that his troops would have to punch man-size holes in thick masonry walls and that there was a lot more bang for the buck in the big rocket warheads than in the lighter, more convenient, but less destructive LAAW warheads.

As soon as 2/5's commander had listed his needs, he turned the task of gathering all the weapons and munitions over to his can-do executive officer, Major John Salvati. Then Cheatham

An Alpha/1/1 rifle squad uses an M48 tank as cover and concealment as it sweeps northeast down a side street adjacent to the MACV Compound. *Official USMC Photo by Staff Sergeant Jack Harlan*

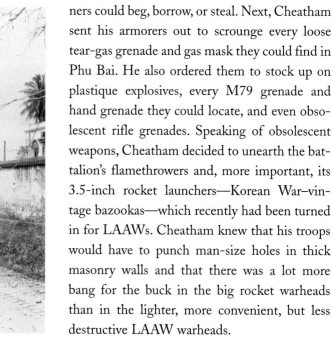

An Army M42 Duster patrols the streets near MACV. The dual-40mm gun array, designed for antiaircraft work aboard World War II–vintage U.S. Navy aircraft carriers, was loved by ground troops because it could take down roughly everything it could reach. *Official USMC Photo by Sergeant William L. Dickman*

By February 3, nearly two thousand civilian refugees had made their way to the vicinity of southern Hue in Marine hands. Every sweep, like the one supported on February 3 by this M48 tank, resulted in new swarms of Vietnamese fleeing Communist-held areas. The civilians received rudimentary screening to root out Communist infiltrators, were given whatever immediate medical care they required, and were turned over to South Vietnamese authorities for feeding and evacuation. *Official USMC Photo by Sergeant William L. Dickman*

holed up in a quiet place to spend the hours he had left in Phu Bai poring over the field manuals.

Major Salvati unearthed 3.5-inch rocket launchers 2/5 and other Marine battalions had stored at Phu Bai, and he scrounged plenty of munitions. He quickly learned that there was a temporary countrywide shortage of hand grenades and that no amount of fast talking, begging, or threats could set it right in the allotted time. Though Salvati had talked Cheatham into allowing him to accompany the convoy into Hue—Salvati was nearing the end of his field tour and had seen no direct combat as yet—he agreed to remain in Phu Bai an extra day so he could scrounge more hand grenades and whatever else he thought the battalion would need.

While the regimental and battalion operations officers pieced together detailed plans, the regimental and battalion personnel officers, Alpha/1/1's first sergeant, and 2/5's first sergeants were hard at work scrounging up more replacements for the many infantrymen who had been killed or wounded in Hue since

Bravo/1/1 was thrown into clearing operations as soon as it reached Hue on the afternoon of February 3. These Bravo Company Marines quickly waded into a fight with an NVA .51-caliber machine gun that caught them on the wrong side of a masonry wall. *Official USMC Photo by Sergeant Bruce Atwell*

A 106mm recoilless rifle team attached to 1/1 moves into position, takes aim, and is beaten to the draw by a Communist RPG or 75mm recoilless rifle round. Counted among the wounded is combat photographer Sergeant Bruce Atwell, who shot up his film on the treatment of wounded until he, too, received care. *Official USMC Photos by Sergeant Bruce A. Atwell*

The two M48 tanks assigned to the 2/5 assault wait on Truong Dinh Street, in the shadow of the University compound, for the assault to begin. *Official USMC Photo by Sergeant William L. Dickman*

A 3.5-inch rocket is hoisted to the Hue University roof as 2/5 revs up its preparations for the late-afternoon assault on the Public Health complex and Treasury. The Hotel/2/5 Marine holding the rope, twenty-four-year-old Corporal James Hedger, was killed in action the next day, February 4. *Official USMC Photo*

January 31. As it had in numerous emergencies in the past, the adage that "every Marine is a rifleman" was applied, so in addition to Marines who were reaching the end of the normal replacement pipeline from the States, the replacement contingent bound for Hue on February 3 would include many motor mechanics, drivers, cooks, bakers, clerks, and rear-area technicians of every variety—and, not to be forgotten, volunteers of every stripe. The stripping of the rear-echelon technicians was particularly brutal in 1/1, whose command group was scheduled to turn the three attached companies of 2/5 back to the 2/5 command group that afternoon. Once that was accomplished, 1/1 would be down to just one company in Hue, Alpha/1/1. Inasmuch as none of Gravel's other three infantry companies could be spared from duties elsewhere, a thinly manned new provisional company called Bravo/1/1 had to be built from part of the real Bravo/1/1 command group,

casual replacements, small levies from all of 1/1's infantry companies, and mainly from 1/1's head-quarters-and-service company.

*

The 1st Marines commander, Colonel Stan Hughes, officially assumed operational control of 2/5 at 1220, as the 1st Marines and 2/5 command groups left Phu Bai. The convoy also included the company of Bravo/1/1, the last dozen Alpha/1/1 stragglers, the platoon of Golf/2/5 used as convoy escort on February 1, a huge low-boy cargo truck carrying 2/5's six 106mm recoilless rifles mounted on mechanical mules, several 6x6 trucks filled with replacements, and two more army M42 40mm Dusters.

The drive to Hue along Highway 1 was rapid, and no delays were experienced. Though the convoy was cumbersome and vulnerable, the only measures the enemy took against it were sporadic sniper fire and several mortar rounds that landed far off target.

One of a pair of M50 Ontos 106mm recoilless rifle carriers to reach Hue on February 2 rushes south along Highway 1 to support a pre-assault clearing operation by Fox/2/5 between the highway and Ly Thuong Kiet Street. The Ontos looks armored, but the outer skin cannot stop a machine-gun bullet, so the exceedingly lethal weapon is rarely used if there is a chance it can be taken under heavy enemy fire. *Courtesy of Alexander Kandic*

Nearing the city, Ernie Cheatham ordered the drivers to increase the speed of their vehicles. The column roared across the exposed canefield causeway and right up the heavily built-up blocks of Highway 1 to MACV. The convoy's trail jeep pulled in at 1258.

*

At 1300, February 3, 2/5 officially resumed operational control of Fox, Golf, and Hotel companies, and 1/1 officially took operational control of the scratch Bravo/1/1. The regimental command post moved into the MACV Compound, the 1/1 command group remained at MACV, and the 2/5 command group set up in Hue University.

At 1330, Gravel and Cheatham received their orders from Regiment. The upshot of the formal operations order was that the 1st Marines regimental assault southwest of Highway 1 was to commence as soon as Marine infantry companies and their supports could close on the line of departure—later that very afternoon. Unofficially, Colonel Stan Hughes, a rough-hewn Navy Cross holder who said little and did much, simply told Cheatham, "Go dig the enemy out," and to call on Regiment for *any* help he thought he needed.

*

The three basic steps for conducting combat in a built-up area are: isolate the battlefield, seize footholds, and conduct a systematic clearing operation.

The Marine and ARVN units in Hue had no control over the first "must," which was in the hands of headquarters controlling events at a regional level. By February 3, the senior ARVN and U.S. headquarters and the divisions they controlled in the I Corps Military Region were not yet sufficiently recovered from the onset of Tet to commit the forces that would be needed to isolate Hue from the outside. Nevertheless, the NVA's apparent ignorance of step 1 had allowed the 1st ARVN Division and Task Force X-Ray to go directly to step 2 on January 31.

Around MACV, 1/1's ongoing company-size battles from the afternoon of January 31 through the forenoon of February 3 were still part of step 2, the consolidation of the foothold. The proposed 1st Marines attack southwest of Highway 1, set to begin on the afternoon of February 3, was to be the beginning of the systematic clearing operation south of the Perfume. North and south of the Perfume, the ARVN and the Marines would be mounting clearing operations from the inside out before their senior headquarters had an opportunity to isolate the city from the outside. It remained to be seen if this serendipitous scenario would be successful, for the NVA retained the option of isolating the city from the outside by seizing or interdicting the Marines' as-yet-unsecured lifeline—Highway 1—from Phu Bai all the way to MACV.

As preparations for the afternoon attack mounted, Task Force X-Ray informed Colonel Hughes that the I ARVN Corps commander had done what might have been the next best thing to sending large units of combat troops to

This Ontos has taken up a partially shielded overwatch position on a side street. Nearby are at least two corpses and a wrecked handcart. The near corpse appears to be a Buddhist monk or nun. *Courtesy of Alexander Kandic*

The Fox/2/5 advance toward Ly Thuong Kiet Street from Highway 1 was accompanied by a Marine flame tank that does not show up on any records available to the author. Here the flame tank—known affectionately as a "Zippo"—moves southwest across Highway 1 from MACV and onto the bloody block of Tran Cao Van Street that figured so prominently in Fox/2/5's February 1 baptism. *Courtesy of Alexander Kandic*

isolate Hue from the outside. On the afternoon of February 3, the ARVN general lifted all restrictions on fire support south of the Perfume River. Hughes' Marines were thus free to call upon any available supporting-arms agency, no matter how destructive its output. This opened the way for on-call support by all manner of artillery, up to 8-inch howitzers, naval gunfire, and, if the weather cleared, tactical aircraft.

*

The 1st Marines' operational plan was simple in the extreme: the Marine infantry companies assigned to Hue were to line up from the Perfume River's southern bank for a distance of four blocks, one company per block. Right to left were Golf/2/5 (between the river and Le Loi Street), Hotel/2/5 (Le Loi to Truong Dinh Street), Fox/2/5 (Truong Dinh to Tran Cao Van Street), and Alpha/1/1 (Tran Cao Van to Nguyen Tri Phuong Street). Bravo/1/1 would be the reserve and would also be on call to screen Alpha/1/1's open right flank as well as defend MACV or clear buildings in the main battle force's rear.

Now well down the block of Tran Cao Van southwest of Highway 1, the Zippo unleashes a stream of flame at one of the buildings as Fox/2/5 machine gunners look on. *Courtesy of Alexander Kandic*

This appears to be an overhead view of the same burst of flame seen in the previous photo. *Official USMC Photo by Sergeant William L. Dickman*

To start with, as 2/5's three companies prepared to jump off at 1345, Alpha/1/1 was tied up in clearing operations near MACV and would not be able to reach its line of departure until the morning of February 4. This would place a heavy burden on Fox Company, whose left flank would

be vulnerable to fire from two large, tall NVA-held buildings in the Alpha/1/1 sector, Le Loi Elementary School and Jeanne d'Arc Private Girls' High School. Moreover, Fox/2/5 had to clear half a block of small buildings between Highway 1 and Ly Thuong Kiet Street just to reach its line of departure, so Hotel/2/5's left flank might be vulnerable to fire from across Tran Cao Van until Fox/2/5 came abreast. The commanders were aware of these shortcomings, but they felt they had to go on the offensive that afternoon to

Opposite views of the February 3 battlefield: (1) Hue University compound—Hotel/2/5 jump-off position with Golf/2/5 in reserve; (2) University chemistry lab and music room—Fox/2/5 jump-off position; (3) Public Health complex; (4) Treasury; (5) Le Loi Elementary School main building; (6) a low building of the Le Loi complex set in on a dogleg in Ly Thuong Kiet Street; (7) the corner of the MACV Compound at Highway 1 and Tran Cao Van.

Hotel/2/5 Marines support the assault on the Public Health complex with rifle fire and M79 40mm grenades fired from upper-story windows on the southwestern side of the University overlooking Ly Thuong Kiet Street. *Official USMC Photos*

offset any plans the Communist commanders might be setting in motion against MACV. As a hedge, Cheatham had Golf/2/5 stage into the University courtyard as battalion reserve. It would go into action in its less-built-up zone as soon as Alpha/1/1 went into the line in the morning.

So, with Ernie Cheatham eyeballing the battlefield from an upper-story window of Hue University overlooking Ly Thuong Kiet Street, Hotel/2/5 and Fox/2/5 prepared to step off toward six solid city blocks of NVA-manned masonry buildings, many two stories tall, some—such as the Treasury—literal fortresses. Two M48s were parked on Truong Dinh Street for use as needed, as were the two Ontos 106mm carriers that had arrived in Hue with Hotel Company.

In Ernie Cheatham's studies at Phu Bai, it had become clear that the way to move through urban terrain was to seize one building at a time through an unyielding application of "cover-and-search" tactics—a combination of target suppression from a base of fire and swift assault of the objective building by a maneuver element. Thus, in the classic manner of infantry attacks, one platoon of Hotel/2/5 was to suppress enemy fire from the upper stories and roof of the University, while another platoon attacked at street level, clearing one building at a time until all the day's objectives had been seized. The third platoon would be held in reserve, for use as needed in target suppression or exploitation of the assault.

Captain Mike Downs' Fox/2/5, which needed to filter and blast its way through the buildings between Highway 1 and Ly Thuong Kiet Street, was initially to support Hotel/2/5's attack by placing flanking fire on Hotel's objectives and suppressing enemy fire from the formidable building it would be facing directly

A Marine rifleman at street level scans upper stories across the way for snipers or RPG gunners who might take the M48 tank under fire as it peeks out from Truong Dinh Street to support the Hotel/2/5 and Fox/2/5 assaults. For all that they look invulnerable, tanks are highly dependent on infantrymen to serve as their eyes and ears when they are buttoned up, especially in close terrain and when enemy troops occupy overhead positions. *Official USMC Photo*

This 2005 photograph shows the Hotel/2/5 February 3, 1968, battlefield. A Hotel/2/5 platoon was ordered to charge out of the entryway and across the street. That's all there was to it. *Courtesy of Colonel Chuck Meadows*

This 2005 view directly down Ly Thuong Kiet Street shows why it was so difficult to cross from the University (left) to the Public Health complex (right): at the end of the second block, at the intersection of Ly Thuong Kiet and Tran Cao Van, is a low building built on a dogleg. An NVA .51-caliber machine gun set up somewhere in the low building had clear aim all the way down Ly Thuong Kiet to beyond the University. Even smoke cover could not hamper the accuracy of the gunners in such a narrow fire zone.
Courtesy of Colonel Chuck Meadows

The Treasury building in 2005.
Courtesy of Colonel Chuck Meadows

Fox/2/5 occupied the University chemistry lab and music room, shown in this 2005 photo. The assault platoon jumped off from a break in the fence and low wall that is not shown here. The .51-caliber machine gun set in at the low building to the Marines' left (right in the photo) was much closer than it was to Hotel/2/5, and it had a much bigger effect on the Fox platoon's ability to get across a relatively narrow street. *Courtesy of Colonel Chuck Meadows*

across Ly Thuong Kiet, the National Treasury. As soon as Hotel/2/5 had taken down its initial objective—a low building fronting Ly Thuong Kiet—Fox/2/5 was to attack straight across the street and seize the fortresslike Treasury.

It took two hours for Fox/2/5 to get into position opposite the Treasury and adjacent Post Office. In that time, 3.5-inch rocket launchers were distributed to Marines who knew how to fire them, and everyone received a gas mask.

Ammunition of all types was distributed, and all hands received a fair share of the limited supply of hand grenades, including tear-gas grenades.

The lead fire team of Hotel/2/5's 2d Platoon jumped off against the low structures fronting the Public Health Complex at 1545. Captain Ron Christmas had reasoned that the best way to get troops across a street that was under enemy observation was to fill the street with smoke, thus obscuring the enemy's vista. So the first thing the attacking platoons and Hotel/2/5's 60mm mortars did was "pop smoke"—heave smoke grenades and fire smoke rounds into Ly Thuong Kiet Street. There was a steady breeze off the river, to the right, so the smoke tended to blow toward the left, across the

front of the Treasury and Post Office buildings and more or less into the faces of the NVA manning Le Loi Elementary School. That should have done the job, but the NVA were not slackers. They fired into the smoke—blindly, to be sure, but quite effectively. Hotel/2/5's lead fire team piled back into the University building.

The 81mm and 60mm mortars set in and near the University courtyard were put into action, albeit against targets beyond the enemy front line, which was only just across the street. Even so, the 81mm mortar gunners had to employ extraordinary skill to fire at ranges far less than those their weapons were designed to reach.

A platoon each from Fox/2/5 and Hotel/2/5 stepped out into Ly Thuong Kiet Street at 1545, the first making for the two-story Treasury and the second making for a one-story building fronting the Public Health complex. Direct support was provided by two M48s deployed on Truong Dinh Street, the company boundary. The plan going in was that, alternating turns, each tank would roll briefly up to the head of Truong Dinh and fire its cupola-mounted .50-caliber machine gun and 90mm main gun at either the Public Health complex or Le Loi Elementary, which dominated Ly Thuong Kiet from Fox/2/5's left rear.

The first tank fired its .50-cal at the nearest Public Health building, but the crew's ardor was quelled by a hail of .51-caliber bullets from the school and an RPG that struck the glacis plate at an oblique angle and dazed the driver.

Hotel's 2d Platoon made it into the nearest Public Health building at 1758 and had cleared it by 1855, but the Fox platoon was rocked back on its heels by heavy fire from the Treasury, to its front, and Le Loi Elementary, to its left rear. When the Fox platoon stopped its fruitless attack at 1924, the Hotel platoon was forced to withdraw back to the University for the night. The Fox platoon left two Marines in the street. The first was a comrade who had been wounded, and the second was a volunteer from the battalion rear who had joined Fox Company the previous after-

noon. The volunteer was shot dead trying to bring in the old hand. It took care and patience to recover the two, one dead and the other alive. Alas, the old hand died the next day in Phu Bai.

The tanks, which alternated firing runs to the bitter end, expended a total of twenty 90mm and four hundred .50-caliber rounds against the Public Health building, Treasury, and Le Loi Elementary, but without apparent effect. Two RPGs struck one of them, and one RPG struck the other. After that, both tanks were withdrawn by their dazed and fearful crewmen. Everyone knew that tanks attract fire, but the February 3 action demonstrated that tanks in a city attract fire from more kinds of places and more directions—including overhead—than tanks in the open.

The first afternoon of the Hue offensive showed everyone involved the way it was going to go—cat-and-mouse, blow and counterblow—for the entire six-city-block assault between Ly Thuong Kiet Street and the 1st Marines' current objective, the Hue Municipal Power Station, which was one block beyond the adjacent Thua Thien Provincial Prison (in Fox/2/5's zone) and the Thua Thien Provincial Administrative Center (on Hotel/2/5's zone). Taking back those government buildings would be far from a true liberation of southern Hue, but it would be a rare American military response to a politically motivated Communist operation.

*

A 2005 view of the Ly Thuong Kiet intersection with Truong Dinh. The tanks peeked out from Truong Dinh, at left, and fired at the Treasury (center) or the Public Health complex (out of sight to right rear). No one realized that the most important target was the building on the dogleg, straight down Ly Thuong Kiet. *Courtesy of Colonel Chuck Meadows*

February 4

The 2d Battalion, 5th Marines, broke the code on February 4.

Fox/2/5 and Hotel/2/5 were slated to jump off across Ly Thuong Kiet Street once again at 0700, February 4. As before, Fox was charged with seizing the Treasury, and Hotel/2/5's objective was the Public Health complex.

During the night, Captain Ron Christmas realized a grave tactical error he had committed in preparing for the February 3 afternoon attack. Rather than establishing the strongest possible base of fire, employing the company's M60 machine guns, Christmas had allowed the M60 teams to remain attached to the rifle platoons. The result was that bush-trained machine gunners had instinctively employed their potent 7.62mm weapons in the manner of assault rifles rather than as medium machine guns. On the morning of February 4, Christmas employed most of the tripod-mounted M60s to bolster his company's base of fire on the roof and in the upper-story windows of the University facing the Public Health complex.

Adding appreciably to 2/5's firepower on the morning of February 4 was the commitment

This 2005 photo shows more or less the NVA machine gunners' view up Ly Thuong Kiet Street, from a low window at the dogleg all the way past the University. The Treasury roof, on left, is green, and the University roof, on right, is red. *Courtesy of Colonel Chuck Meadows*

The key to the Hotel/2/5 attack from the University to the Public Health complex was to be raw firepower. Here, a 106mm recoilless rifle is deployed in the Golf/2/5 zone to cover the Hotel Company's right flank against fire from parkland between Le Loi Street and the Perfume River. *Courtesy of Douglas Blayney*

The 106mm recoilless rifle attached to Hotel/2/5 fires a round down Ly Thuong Kiet Street from Hue University's western corner. This photo was taken after the assault, as the 106 is firing at the Treasury in support of the Fox/2/5 assault. *Official USMC Photo by Sergeant William L. Dickman*

The 106 gunners' view down Ly Thuong Kiet, taken hours or even days after the Fox/2/5 crossing. The corner of the Treasury is at right center. Note the discarded 106mm canisters. *Official USMC Photo*

A 2005 photo of the entrance to the former University (now a hotel) at the corner of Le Loi and Ly Thuong Kiet streets. Most Hue veterans visiting the city stay here. *Courtesy of Colonel Chuck Meadows*

of most of Captain Chuck Meadows' Golf/2/5 to the attack-support scheme. Elements of Golf/2/5 were posted with 3.5-inch rocket launchers and tripod-mounted M60s high up and along the southeastern side of the University. Their primary target was Le Loi Elementary School, from which an NVA .51-caliber machine gun had stymied the February 3 attack.

Another twist unique to city fighting had become apparent in the waning hours of February 3. Quite naturally, the 3.5-inch rocket-men had aimed their potent weapons through open windows in the hope of killing people inside enemy-held rooms. The success rate had been stunningly low. The rocketmen had indeed sent their missiles through the windows, but that did little or no good because the rockets did not detonate until they hit something solid. And when they did, the blast was in the direction the rocket was going—away from the NVA manning the windows. Late-night bull sessions resulted in new orders to all the rocketmen. On the morning of February 4, they fired at the front walls of enemy-held buildings, right beneath and beside the windows from which the NVA were firing. That way, the kinetic energy of

Hotel/2/5 Marines dash across an open space as the company filters through the Public Health complex. *Official USMC Photo by Sergeant William L. Dickman*

the rocket blasts caused masonry shards and shrapnel to cut down or at least seriously daze the men firing from the windows.

The Hotel/2/5 dawn attack jumped off under covering fire from many M60s, 3.5-inch rocket launchers, M79 grenades, LAAWs, and twenty-five 81mm mortar rounds directed by Fox/2/5's 81mm forward observer. The 81mm mortar fire missions were particularly nerve-racking in that the nearest targets were actually within the minimum firing range of the mortars. The solution to this anomaly was provided by the mortar platoon commander, Gunnery Sergeant Lawrence Bargaheiser. Located in the University courtyard, the six 81mm tubes were erected on their bipods at virtually vertical elevation, and the rounds were fired with minimum charges for the least possible range. As the rounds were lofted above the University roof, the steady southerly breeze from off the Perfume River carried them just far enough to the southwest to tilt them into the NVA positions for which they were meant. Altogether, it was a masterful performance of technical proficiency.

For all the fire support, however, Hotel's lead platoon ran straight into exactly the sort of fire that had stymied the initial afternoon attacks of February 3; NVA in high buildings fired down into the street, and the .51-caliber in Le Loi Elementary cut the attack off at its knees. NVA in hidden positions southwest of Ly Thuong Kiet who blasted away at the University forced Marines from the windows.

Hotel's attack across Ly Thuong Kiet was getting exactly nowhere until the lance corporal commanding a 106mm recoilless rifle attached to the company approached Captain Christmas with an original idea. (A key to successful command in combat is listening to ideas from all ranks.) The 106 gunner pointed out that the deadliest fire was

coming from way to the left, apparently from a .51-caliber set in low somewhere inside Le Loi Elementary. He also pointed out that the back-blast from his 106 could throw up enough debris to cover a rush across the street. The way the lance corporal had it figured, he and his assistant gunner could roll their 106 into the street on its mechanical mule and fire at the school to suppress or maybe even destroy the machine gun. As soon as the 106 fired, Christmas could mount a platoon or two through the dust and debris thrown up by the backblast. The big advantage was that unlike an attack through smoke, the NVA wouldn't know what was going on until it had already happened.

Christmas asked the lance corporal if he really understood what he was volunteering to do. Yes, the gunner knew. With that, Christmas ordered the lead platoon to cross Ly Thuong Kiet as soon as the 106 fired.

Lieutenant Colonel Ernie Cheatham got wind of the plan and decided to take a personal role in perfecting it. He eased out a side door of the University and advanced up Truong Dinh Street to the intersection with fire-swept Ly Thuong Kiet. There he tucked his 6-foot, 4-inch frame behind a telephone pole and peeked to his left, across Fox/2/5's front, toward Le Loi Elementary. He saw the muzzle flash and the telltale green tracers of a .51-caliber machine gun coming from a window right at street level. Cheatham got down in a kneeling position behind the telephone pole. He noticed that when the machine gun fired at targets on the southwestern side of Ly Thuong Kiet—the side the Treasury and Public Health objectives were on—it fired low. But as the gunner traversed the barrel to lay on targets on the northeast side of the street, the stream of tracer rose. The gun seemed to be obstructed by something. Cheatham became convinced that the gun fired so high to its right that there was no way he could be hit if he stepped into the street to mark the target for the 106 crew.

Cheatham went back into the University courtyard to lay out a plan of action with the 106 crew. Essentially, they were to bounce their mechanical mule down some low steps to the western corner of the University, at Le Loi and Ly Thuong Kiet streets, and he would mark the target with tracer rounds, the only type of ammunition most senior Marine commanders carried, precisely for situations like the one at hand. The gunner agreed to the plan.

Marines from Hotel/2/5's 3d Platoon carry a wounded comrade to the rear for medical treatment.
Official USMC Photo

A Hotel/2/5 3.5-inch rocket team helps to evacuate a woman and child from one of the many buildings within the Public Health complex. Note the 3.5-inch rocket at the Marine's side. *Official USMC Photo by Sergeant William L. Dickman*

A Marine M48 main battle tank took part in preparing the way for 1/1's February 4 assault into the block containing Jeanne d'Arc Private Girls' High School and Le Loi Elementary School. But once the troops entered the tangle of buildings, the tanks could be more of a liability than an asset. *Official USMC Photo by Corporal John Pennington*

The M79 grenade launcher's 40mm projectile was an excellent weapon in close terrain, though it would not arm until it had gone beyond its own blast radius from the grenadier. An experienced grenadier could instantly compute the distance and firing angle to anything he could see. *Official USMC Photo by Lance Corporal R. J. Smith*

A pair of snipers attached to Alpha/1/1 are perched high up in a building overlooking NVA positions in the Jeanne d'Arc school. The Marine on the left is armed with an M14 semiautomatic rifle that fires a lethally powerful 7.62mm round. *Official USMC Photo by Corporal John Pennington*

Cheatham went back to the telephone pole and sighted in on the target. He couldn't quite get a round on it, so he leaned out for a better shot. His next round hit near the target, and the target tried to hit him. The green tracer snapped and cracked right over Cheatham's head, but the gunner could not hit the tall battalion commander.

True to their word, the 106 gunner and his assistant bounced their mechanical mule down the steps and positioned it on the sidewalk. Instantly, as the gunners turned the recoilless rifle's barrel to bear on the school building, the NVA machine gun traversed to bear on them.

Cheatham fired his M16 marking rounds right at the target window. The 106 gunner squatted down behind the sight and twisted aiming wheels while the assistant gunner loaded a high-explosive round into the breech. "Fire the fifty!" the gunner called, as if he were practicing gun drill on a stateside range. "Fire the fifty!" the assistant responded as he thumbed a half-inch-thick tracer round into the .50-caliber single-shot spotting rifle set atop the 106mm barrel. The gunner fired

Major John Salvati, the 2/5 executive officer, performed yeoman service during the last few days before his departure for a job on the 1st Marine Division staff. At Phu Bai on February 3, he bullied troops, weapons, and supplies from reluctant superiors, and led the February 4 morning convoy to Hue, where he commandeered tear-gas launchers from reluctant ARVN troops. He fired the tear gas that started the Fox/2/5 assault on the Treasury, then he trained 3.5-inch rocket teams, and he even fired a 3.5-inch rocket under fire while demonstrating his technique to his pupils. *Official USMC Photo by Sergeant William L. Dickman courtesy of Lieutenant Colonel Ralph J. Salvati*

the tracer round and watched it strike near, but not on, the spot Cheatham's tracer was hitting.

The gunner corrected his aim. "Fire the fifty!" he yelled. "Fire the fifty!" the assistant gunner yelled back. The second marking round curved down along Ly Thuong Kiet and struck closer to the target, but not quite on it.

The 106 gunner corrected his aim once again. "Fire the fifty!" he yelled for the third time. "Fire the fifty!" the assistant gunner responded. The third .50-caliber tracer struck the northern face of the low building on the dogleg, right in among Cheatham's M16 marking rounds.

Instantly, the gunner yelled, "Fire the 106!" The assistant gunner responded, "Fire the 106!" And . . . Ba-ROOM! The round roared down Ly Thuong Kiet Street toward the school, and a huge billow of debris and dust spread across the front of the University. As it did, the 106 gunners retreated into the University courtyard, and the assault rifle platoon once again charged toward the low buildings fronting the Public Health complex. The 106 round destroyed the NVA .51-caliber machine-gun position.

Two Hotel/2/5 Marines were wounded during the rush across Ly Thuong Kiet, but the pla-

toon once again established a strong toehold inside the Public Health complex. The low buildings fronting the Public Health building itself were thoroughly cleared in a matter of minutes.

*

While a platoon each from Alpha/1/1 and Bravo/1/1 were detailed to secure more ground and facilities around MACV, the rest of Lieutenant Colonel Mark Gravel's small 1/1 contingent was committed early to draw abreast 2/5 at Ly Thuong Kiet Street on the block between Tran Cao Van and Nguyen Tri Phuong streets. Their main objectives were Jeanne d'Arc High School and Le Loi Elementary. Unfortunately, both were mazes of buildings honeycombed with NVA fighting positions. Progress in close-in room-to-room, floor-to-floor fighting was slow. A Marine M48 helped get the jackleg battalion into the first buildings, but from there only brute force, blood, and bravery sustained the advance.

Halfway through the block, 1/1 ran into a major NVA defensive sector centered on the huge square compound occupied by the Jeanne d'Arc school. The Marines managed to enter the

This 106mm recoilless rifle has been laboriously carried to an upper-story window of Hue University overlooking Ly Thuong Kiet Street. It will be able to fire just one round because its backblast will certainly blow the room apart. Once the gunner has brought the sights to bear and fired a marker round, the gun section attaches a 20-foot lanyard made from string to the trigger and evacuates down the hall. The single round strikes dead on the Treasury building facing Fox/2/5. *Official USMC Photo*

The Treasury following Fox/2/5's successful February 4 assault. *Official USMC Photo courtesy of Colonel Chuck Meadows*

long building on the northeastern side of the complex, but they were unable to advance across the exposed quadrangle or through the northwestern and southwestern wings of the buildings. By 0900 the advance was stopped, and both sides were exchanging small-arms fire, 3.5-inch rockets, LAAWs, and RPGs.

Sergeant Alfredo Gonzalez, the platoon sergeant of Alpha/1/1's 2d Platoon, was a young man who reveled in close combat. He was an absolutely fearless, ferocious fighter, more than willing to

take responsibility for leading direct assaults on the enemy. Usually, when facing the enemy, the twenty-one-year-old Texan showed a huge, toothy grin. At about 0900, February 4, Sergeant Gonzalez collected an armload of LAAW rockets and climbed to the second floor of the Marine-held building in the Jeanne d'Arc complex. In an attempt to get NVA soldiers to reveal their positions and perhaps bolt into the open, Gonzalez moved from window to window, firing LAAWs into the enemy-held rooms facing the quadrangle. He was especially intent upon engaging NVA RPG teams. While the NVA had their heads down, several of the Marines Gonzalez was supporting tried to attack across the open area, but the NVA recovered and threw the Marines back with intense fire. Sergeant Gonzalez went back to work on the NVA positions with his collection of LAAWs, but the NVA finally figured out what the Marine platoon sergeant had in mind. At 0905, a patient NVA RPG team caught him in one of the windows and fired right at him. Sergeant Gonzalez was struck by the RPG in the midriff

As Fox/2/5 scoured the square block containing the Treasury, Post Office, and sundry other buildings and homes, at least thirty well-dressed Vietnamese civilians emerged from hiding. They were gathered up and escorted to MACV for processing. *Courtesy of Alexander Kandic*

A late afternoon shooting incident directed at the 1st Marines command post resulted in several casualties on both sides. Note that several civilians wearing helmets and flak jackets have turned up to help Bravo/1/1 Marines load the casualties aboard an ambulance. *Official USMC Photo by Sergeant Bruce Atwell*

and mortally wounded. Sergeant Alfredo Gonzalez would be awarded a posthumous Medal of Honor in recognition of all his singular acts of heroism on the way to and inside Hue.

The room-by-room advance continued.

*

Captain Mike Downs' Fox/2/5 used a different approach to assault the Treasury. Major John Salvati, the 2/5 executive officer, arrived early from Phu Bai with fresh reinforcements, supplies, ammunition, and an assortment of weapons and gear. Among the latter were more than enough gas masks to equip Fox/2/5—but no tear gas. This Salvati set right by taking it away from a unit of ARVN troops sitting on their heels in a compound near MACV. He supplied Fox/2/5 with pack-mounted tear-gas pellet launchers.

The tear gas was fired a moment after noon. As the gas was carried down Ly Thuong Kiet by the breeze off the river, Fox/2/5's 3d Platoon staged three rolling squad rushes. The Marines could not see much through sight-impeding gas-mask lenses, but they confidently thundered into the Treasury—right, left, and up a narrow flight of stairs. Many NVA on the ground floor fled out the back, while most on the second floor stood, fought, and died. Of eighteen Fox/2/5 Marines wounded in the assault, about half were evacuated, several were treated on the spot and released, and several never requested medical care because they wanted to stay with their buddies.

The Post Office fell to Fox/2/5 without a fight as soon as the Treasury had been taken down.

So February 4 was the red-letter day in southern Hue. The 1st Marines' offensive had gotten off to a ragged start, but it had achieved its first physical breakthrough and an even more important psychological breakthrough. City fighting was damn hard, and it was nothing like bush combat, but Marines of all ranks and stations learned on February 4 that taking down buildings and whole blocks of buildings was something they could do with the proper amount of preparation and the usual dose of bravery.

By day's end, Hotel/2/5 had cleared the entire city block bounded by Le Loi, Ly Thuong Kiet, Truong Dinh, and Le Dinh Duong streets; Fox/2/5 had firm possession of the Treasury and Post Office; and the two weakened companies of 1/1 had made a firm lodgment about halfway into the Jeanne d'Arc school grounds.

Indeed, when NVA holed up in buildings between the river and Le Loi Street attacked Hotel/2/5 with heavy fire at 1755, one of the company's platoons crossed Le Loi and Le Dinh Duong streets to seize a large, opulent house overlooking the river. A Golf/2/5 platoon then attacked southwest from Highway 1 across undefended parkland all the way to another house on the southwestern side of Le Dinh Duong Street. This allowed the Hotel platoon in the opulent house to seize the French Cultural Center, also southwest of Le Dinh Duong, between the two houses. The entire evolution was bloodless.

At 1940, two hours after a second resupply convoy battled across the Phu Cam Canal's An Cuu Bridge, word reached MACV that Communist sappers had finally blown the bridge. This isolated Hue by road from the south, but the damage had been done in the five days the bridge had remained intact, and the Marine holdings in southern Hue remained accessible via the Hue LCU Ramp and from the air. It was a blow to convenience, but not much of a blow in fact.

*

The An Cuu Bridge over the Phu Cam Canal, near the southern extremity of southern Hue, was blown up by Communist sappers at 1940, February 4. The loss of the bridge inconvenienced Marines in Hue, but it in no way endangered them. *Colonel Chuck Meadows Collection*

Battle-hardened Marines learned early in their combat tours to catch up on sleep wherever and whenever possible. Rare was the day they had access to real furniture, four walls, and a roof. *Courtesy of Alexander Kandic*

February 5

The 1st Marines' regimental objective remained the same on February 5: 1/1 and 2/5 were to continue their attacks to secure the Thua Thien Provincial Prison and the Thua Thien Provincial Administrative Center. There were four long blocks between the objectives and the line 2/5 held during the night of February 4–5, and there was no reason to suspect that the NVA soldiers holding the scores of masonry buildings in between would be any more willing to give them up than they had been willing to give up the Treasury or Public Health complex.

Golf/2/5 Marines prepare for their February 5 morning assault on Hue's upscale Cercle Sportif. The man in silhouette, using the radio handset, is Captain Chuck Meadows. *Courtesy of Douglas Blayney*

Cheatham's 2/5 was ready to go on, but Gravel's 1/1 had just about run out of steam. Despite being brought partly back to strength by the arrival of its officers and nearly a full platoon of stragglers, Alpha/1/1 was basically used up by the morning of February 5, and an entire platoon had been detached to outpost the battalion's southern flank. Bravo/1/1 was composed mainly of pickup squads of headquarters technicians and weapons specialists; it was not completely viable as a tactical unit. The Marines who remained operational in Gravel's demibattalion gave it their all, but the task of clearing the enormous Jeanne d'Arc complex was beyond their capabilities, and little progress was made there on February 4 or February 5.

On the other hand, Ernie Cheatham was a happy man on the morning of February 5. He had expected Fox/2/5 to remain stymied in front of the Treasury well into February 5. The day before, Fox/2/5 had taken the Treasury, and Hotel/2/5's and Golf/2/5's late-afternoon exploitive attack across Le Dinh Duong Street had led to the bloodless occupation of the French Cultural Center, on the northwestern side of Le Loi Street. Cheatham now hoped that the quick, cheap February 4 victories heralded a softening of NVA opposition.

There were ample indications that the NVA were preparing to defend the city blocks in front of 2/5 in considerable strength. During the evening of February 4, a trickle of civilian refugees arriving from the southwest had turned into a

flood amounting to several hundred of Hue's Vietnamese citizens—and five American teachers and medical workers. The Vietnamese civilians had been passed on to the Vietnamese civil authorities, but the Americans had been questioned at length in the hope of turning up possible leads regarding NVA intentions and plans. The news appeared grim. The NVA and VC were fortifying the Hue Central Hospital complex in great strength because, apparently, scores of non-ambulatory wounded Communist soldiers were being treated in beds from which civilians had been forcibly extricated.

*

The day's fighting south of the Perfume kicked off at 0530, on the southern flank of the 1/1 sector. Here, several NVA were killed as they approached Alpha/1/1 Marines getting ready to move out of the Jeanne d'Arc Student Center.

Hotel/2/5 led 2/5's efforts with a sweep to completely clear the area around a home one of the platoons had captured the previous afternoon. This was done, with alacrity, against light opposition. Likewise, Fox/2/5's first action of the day was scouring once again the area between the rear of the Treasury and Post Office buildings and Le Dinh Duong Street. When the original holdings had been recleared, Fox/2/5 and Hotel/2/5 advanced cautiously into new territory to the southwest.

At 0829, Fox/2/5 Marines checking a building the NVA had given up without a fight

discovered a handful of live U.S. Air Force officers and enlisted men who had been hiding there since the morning of January 31. This building and these men were what Fox/2/5 platoon had been sent to secure and a rescue at great cost and without success as soon as it had arrived in Hue on February 1.

By 0834, Fox/2/5's right platoon had advanced an entire block without opposition and was in possession of the neighborhood municipal police station at the end of Truong Dinh Street.

By 0840, Golf/2/5 had conducted an unimpeded advance through the riverfront parkland northwest of Le Loi Street, then fought its way into the Cercle Sportif, a ritzy club that had been a cultural stronghold of Hue's French and

Marines backed by truckloads of ammunition and heavy weapons stage for the beginning of 2/5's February 5 assault. *Official USMC Photos*

During the attack on the Cercle Sportif, a Golf/2/5 Marine peers into the smoke of battle at a thoroughly out-of-place echo from Hue's French past. *Courtesy of Douglas Blayney*

From the deck beside the Cercle Sportif's yacht slips, Golf/2/5 Marines had a clear view of smoke rising from the embattled Citadel of Hue, where the 1st ARVN Division was retaking lost ground. *Courtesy of Douglas Blayney (who was wounded in the hand and evacuated to Phu Bai on February 5)*

Lieutenant Colonel Ernie Cheatham stands tall in the middle of Le Loi Street to direct an Ontos against NVA strongpoints holding up the 2/5 advance. *Courtesy of Lieutenant Colonel John Salvati*

A 2/5 M60 team member laden with belts of 7.62mm ammunition wisely scours the urban terrain he must cross when his unit is ordered to resume the advance. *Official USMC Photo by Sergeant William L. Dickman*

Vietnamese upper classes. The roof of the Cercle Sportif afforded Golf/2/5 a wonderful all-around view. The Perfume River was just to the north, and the Citadel, from which thick columns of smoke rose, was in plain view.

Also in plain view from the roof of the Cercle Sportif was 2/5's obvious next main objective, the multiblock Hue Central Hospital complex, a rabbit warren of countless buildings of all sizes and shapes. But before the attack into the Hospital could commence, Hotel/2/5 and Fox/2/5 had to fight their way abreast of Golf/2/5's advanced position.

Hotel/2/5's advance to the southwest down the narrow but heavily built-up residential block in the center of the 2/5 zone took only a little longer than the stunning advances by the flank companies. At 0850, Hotel/2/5's lead platoon entered the Hue University Library, between the Cercle Sportif and the municipal police station.

By only 0900, February 5, 2/5's entire objective area for the day had fallen with only minimal opposition. By that time the entire battalion was arrayed along Le Thanh Ton Street, an east–west thoroughfare that cut across the southwest-facing battalion front at a 45-degree angle between the river, on Golf/2/5's right, and Tran Cao Van Street,

This bloated and bloody Vietnamese civilian has probably been lying in the street since the NVA first took possession of southern Hue on January 31. *Courtesy of Alexander Kandic*

on Fox/2/5's left. Though 1/1 was stalled a full block to Fox/2/5's left rear, Ernie Cheatham decided to keep going as long as he could. He felt he had the enemy on the run, and this was certainly no time to wait for 1/1 to clear the opposition on its front and advance abreast. So without further ado, as soon as all three of his companies were in possession of a 400-meter line along Le Thanh Ton, Cheatham ordered them to advance into the vast network of barracks-type buildings comprising the Hue Central Hospital complex.

As soon as Hotel/2/5 jumped off toward the Hospital, across Le Thanh Ton Street, NVA soldiers strongly emplaced in buildings across the company's front put up resistance every bit as stiff as any 2/5 had faced in Hue.

Fox/2/5's initial advance into an empty triangle of parkland south of Le Thanh Ton was

A Hotel/2/5 rifleman, .45-caliber pistol at the ready, prods a pile of straw to find out if a Communist straggler has taken refuge there. Note that this Marine carries two LAAW antitank rockets. *Official USMC Photo by Sergeant William L. Dickman*

This Marine sniper searches through his telescopic sight for an NVA sniper across from his upper-story position. *Official USMC Photo by Lance Corporal R. J. Smith*

uncontested. But as soon as the company pivoted back to the southwest to face the Hospital complex across Nguyen Thai Street, the NVA who were already battling Hotel/2/5 stopped it.

In addition to facing renewed NVA resistance to its front, Fox/2/5 was hampered by the need to watch its open left flank. Alpha/1/1 was by

Marine riflemen break cover to advance rapidly along an uncontested stretch of a side street. *Official USMC Photo by Sergeant William L. Dickman*

then several hundred meters to Fox/2/5's left rear. When the squad screening the open flank was badly shot up by heavy fire from the open area, another squad was committed. The NVA kept up the pressure, wounded several Marines, and shot at evacuees and their rescuers. At length, after a dozen Marines had been wounded, the hard-bitten Fox/2/5 veterans dislodged the NVA with heavy fire. Of the wounded, only eight accepted treatment; the rest wanted to stay and fight. Three of the men who were treated returned to duty that day, but five had to be evacuated to Phu Bai.

The 1st Marines command post was rocketed at 0920, for the second time in as many days, and the MACV Advisory Team 3 tactical operations center was near-missed by another 122mm rocket. A Marine artillery battery emplaced south of the city fired eighteen 105mm rounds at the suspected rocket site. Results could not be determined, but the rocket fire ceased.

At 1030, the NVA facing Hotel/2/5 and Golf/2/5 were apparently reinforced; NVA fire just about doubled. An 81mm mortar mission mounted to eighty-five rounds against the main source of the fire. Under cover of the mortar barrage and Golf/2/5's base of fire, Hotel/2/5's

A Fox/2/5 rifleman drags a dead NVA soldier from a building that has just fallen into Marine hands. Dead NVA became a fairly common sight as 2/5's February 5 attack progressed. *Courtesy of Alexander Kandic*

Hundreds of southern Hue's traumatized civilians flooded into Marine lines as 2/5 ground forward on February 5. *Official USMC Photo*

right-flank platoon rushed across Nguyen Thai Street and seized an NVA-held building. The rush cost the NVA eight more killed against five Marines wounded and evacuated and three Marines with minor wounds.

The ongoing 2/5 attack stalled for more than two hours, but casualties were nil despite heavy exchanges of fire. Then, at 1240, NVA facing Golf/2/5 on the southwestern side of the Cercle Sportif fired five RPGs and several machine guns that wounded six Marines. In response, Marine gunfire and three 3.5-inch rockets killed six NVA and opened the way for an immediate flank attack into the strongpoint by a Hotel/2/5 squad. This in turn opened the way for Hotel/2/5's seizure of an adjacent building, after which the NVA in a nearby bunker stymied hot pursuit by firing eight RPGs and many automatic weapons at the Marines. In retaliation, the Marines fired fifteen 3.5-inch rockets into the enemy bunker and followed up with an uncontested direct assault. Ten fresh NVA corpses were found in the ruins of the bunker.

In unrelated action to 2/5's left rear, NVA located several hundred meters south of the Jeanne d'Arc complex pumped three RPGs into

A thin-skinned Ontos has been brought up to a semi-covered position to lay fire on an infantry objective ahead. The Ontos provides no real protection for the two crewmen, and the 106mm recoilless rifles have to be loaded by the gunner as he stands outside the vehicle. But 2/5 needed every ounce of fire support it could muster for its bloody but spectacularly successful February 5 assault, and the Ontos crewmen gave it their all despite multiple risks. *Official USMC Photo*

A Marine M48 main battle tank blasts an infantry objective with its powerful 90mm main gun. Tanks firing all along the 2/5 front, wherever they could find a field of fire, were instrumental in the day's successes. *Official USMC Photo*

A Marine probes through the ruins of a home or public building. This was tense, dangerous work, but every room of every building had to be eyeballed before Marines could put it behind them. *Official USMC Photo*

Wherever possible, dead Communist soldiers were dragged to open areas, both to be sure they were really dead and to make searches for intelligence data safer and more efficient. These photos are two views of a covey of NVA killed along Fox/2/5's axis of advance. *Courtesy of Alexander Kandic*

the 1/1 sector, wounding two Marines. An artillery forward observer retaliated by calling in a fire mission by Marine self-propelled 8-inch howitzers located at Phu Bai. The results could not be determined, but the NVA RPG teams in the target area did not resume fire on 1/1.

At 1251, on 2/5's extreme left flank, Fox/2/5 was struck by intense small-arms fire and five RPGs. The Marines returned the small-arms fire in kind, added a dozen M79 fragmentation grenades, and called a thirty-round 60mm mortar mission on the offending structure. The fight turned into a standoff until a Marine Ontos worked its way into a semicovered position from which it could fire its six 106mm ready rounds at the enemy-held building. The Fox/2/5 Marines were off and running toward the objective as soon as the Ontos fired its last round. The dazed NVA survivors were easily driven from the structure, and four freshly killed NVA were found in the rubble.

And so it went. At 1300, on 2/5's left flank, the NVA hit Hotel/2/5 with rifle fire and two rounds from a captured M79. The Marines returned fire, including three M79 rounds, and killed at least one NVA soldier. At the same time, the main body of Alpha/1/1, still mired in the Jeanne d'Arc complex, was engaged by NVA small-arms fire and two RPGs. These Marines responded with a much heavier volume of M16 and M60 fire, plus five LAAWs and twenty 106mm recoilless rifle rounds, and a Marine tank struck the enemy position with fifteen 90mm rounds. One Marine was killed and four were wounded and evacuated. Later, four dead NVA were pulled from the fortified position at the focus of the Marine fire.

Throughout the morning and noon hours, scores and perhaps hundreds of civilians emerged from the rubble of their homes and the many public buildings in the area. At one point a large number of teaching nuns entered Fox/2/5's position from their hiding place in the National Nurses' Training Center, just off 2/5's left flank. The constant stream of civilians forced the Marine company commanders to voluntarily diffuse their sorely needed assets because they felt duty-bound to provide troops to escort the fearful, often-injured refugees out of the battle zone. Worse, though the Marines were pretty much under orders to shoot first and ask questions later, there was a natural tendency for them to withhold fire until they were certain their targets were really hostiles. No one wanted to be responsible for killing a defenseless child.

For about two hours, until 1500, 2/5 stopped to reorganize and take on an ammunition resupply. Pressure on the NVA was maintained—and returned—throughout the break, but no attempts were made to take new ground. At 1500, in what would become one of the most significant efforts of the day, Golf/2/5 attacked southward, across Hotel/2/5's front, right into one of the main hospital buildings. The objective was held in great strength, and Golf/2/5 became embroiled in a foot-by-foot, yard-by-yard, room-by-room battle of wills.

In most cases, whenever a new building or room fell into Marine hands, the only signs of recent NVA occupation were little piles of spent cartridges and, rarely, a blood trail. Civilian patients liberated from medical wards almost invariably gave wordless indications that the NVA were close by, but they made it adequately clear with body language that they were not about to get involved.

At 1600, while waiting for Golf/2/5 to cross its front, Hotel/2/5 was struck by small-arms fire and several RPGs put out by NVA soldiers holding a position practically on top of the opposing

When you get right down to it, most of the battle-hardened Marines who fought in Hue were American teenagers raised in a time when community service was taken for granted. So even in a situation in which helping out a little old lady with a cast on her leg diminished 2/5's lethality and efficiency, the little old lady was going to be rescued by any means at hand, including the arms of a battle-hardened Hotel/2/5 combat grenadier. *Official USMC Photo by Sergeant William L. Dickman*

A Marine combat engineer attached to Hotel/2/5 gingerly checks for a booby-trap device through the clothing of a dead Communist infantryman. The NVA soldier's weapon is an American-made World War II–era .30-caliber M1 carbine. *Official USMC Photo by Sergeant William L. Dickman*

The Marines of 2/5 killed dozens of NVA soldiers on February 5, but they only captured a handful. Combat Marines serving in the Vietnam War rarely saw live NVA. *Official USMC Photo by Sergeant William L. Dickman*

Marine position. As was typical by then, the Hotel/2/5 Marines responded massively to the NVA challenge. More than 1,500 M16 and M60 rounds were expended, as were four 106mm recoilless rifle rounds and six 3.5-inch rockets. For good measure, the Hotel/2/5 Marines threw in a quick assault and secured the NVA position. Seven Marines were wounded and evacuated in this exchange alone, against eight NVA killed and one wounded NVA captured. The Marines also captured two AK-47s, three old American-made carbines, and a pair of RPG launchers.

Also at 1600, on the 2/5 left flank, Fox/2/5 opened an attack on a building in a cultivated field to its left front. As the NVA resistance in front of Fox/2/5 stiffened, the Marines softened the building up with intense small-arms fire supplemented with 106mm fire from an Ontos, 81mm mortar fire, and 3.5-inch rocket fire. Then they attacked. The objective was seized at a loss of two Marines wounded against seven more NVA killed.

Golf/2/5 continued to inch forward into the Hospital complex until the NVA defenders finally broke and ran at 1632. At the end of the ninety-two-minute assault, in which Marine tanks, 106mm recoilless rifles, and 3.5-inch rocket launchers played pivotal roles, Captain Chuck Meadows' company lost five more wounded. The Golf/2/5 Marines found four dead NVA inside the liberated portions of the objective—and thirty wounded patients who appeared to be NVA or

VC. Trucks had to be called up from MACV to transport the wounded prisoners and forty-two assorted NVA weapons to the rear.

A thorough search of the operating rooms in Marine hands revealed signs of heavy recent use. Mounds of bloody waste bandages and numerous other signs revealed that scores and perhaps hundreds of patients had been treated up to as recently as a few hours earlier for all kinds of battle wounds. The search also turned up several dozen insane patients who had been locked inside their ward with barely enough food or water to survive. These poor souls were evacuated to MACV on foot, as were numerous medical patients and others who were obviously not NVA or VC.

At 1645, less than a quarter hour after Golf/2/5 seized its objective, Hotel/2/5 jumped off again, this time to seize a large building between its front and Golf/2/5's left flank. The NVA manning the objective were between the proverbial rock and a hard place. Golf/2/5 was already holding the building to the rear of the objective, and elements of Fox/2/5 had the only other exit, to the southeast, covered. The NVA, who were well dug in, put out intense small-arms and RPG fire, and they would not budge.

The Hotel/2/5 cleanup attack quickly bogged down in the face of relentless resistance. Under pressure from Ernie Cheatham to roll up the NVA, Captain Ron Christmas ran forward across a 35-meters open area to confer with the

A pair of Soviet-pattern RPD light machine guns and a B-40 RPG launcher (foreground) captured in Hue are displayed for Marine cameramen and civilian correspondents. *Official USMC Photo*

troop leaders and see for himself what could be done to get the company moving again. Christmas decided that he needed help from the M48 tank that had accompanied Golf/2/5 to its objective. He returned to his command post and ordered his reserve platoon to work forward, into positions from which it could join the final rush. Then Christmas sprinted across another fire-swept open stretch—this one 70 meters wide—to the tank.

The desperate NVA poured heavy machine-gun fire in the direction of the tank, and both of the RPGs they fired at it struck the frontal glacis plate as Captain Christmas was climbing up in back. With Christmas standing tall behind the turret, directing fire, the M48 fired five 90mm rounds into the NVA-held building. As the tank and Marines manning a base of fire suppressed the enemy fire, the Hotel/2/5 reserve platoon swept in and quickly reduced the opposition with the aid of tear-gas grenades. Three Marines were wounded in this phase of the assault, and the bodies of twelve NVA and many weapons were recovered. Captain Ron Christmas was awarded a Navy Cross.

As the Hotel/2/5 platoons continued to scour the objective under Christmas's direct leadership, previously unperceived NVA manning what turned out to be underground bunkers on three sides of the building opened fire on them. The M48 was brought up to fire its main gun and .50-caliber cupola machine gun into one bunker after another. The surviving NVA bolted from the last bunker, but they were cut down in the open as they sprinted across a street.

Thirteen dead NVA were recovered from the bunkers, for a total of twenty-five NVA killed in the one strongpoint. Strewn throughout the position was the largest haul of NVA weapons captured to date, including many personal weapons, three RPG launchers, and two Chinese-made RPD light machine guns.

At 1700, Alpha/1/1's main body took intense fire from several bunkers in no-man's-land southeast of the Jeanne d'Arc complex. For reasons that never became clear—for they did not launch an assault—the NVA fired an estimated 2,500 rifle and machine-gun rounds and eight RPGs into the Alpha/1/1 lines. The Marines responded with 3,000 M16 and M60 rounds, and they directed the firing of twenty-two 90mm tank rounds, twenty-nine 81mm mortar rounds, and seventy-one 8-inch and two 105mm howitzer rounds. The artillery fire caused several violent secondary explosions in one NVA position. One Marine was killed and eight were wounded and evacuated. Alpha/1/1 claimed nine confirmed kills.

At 1815, capping a successful but costly day, a Fox/2/5 platoon entered the southern portion of a hospital building in its sector. These Marines found five dead NVA and took three prisoners. One of the captives turned out to be the mayor of Hue *and* the Thua Thien Province chief, who had been hiding while clad in a hospital gown.

*

At 1715, the first navy landing craft to reach the embattled city arrived at the Hue LCU Ramp from Danang. With the An Cuu Bridge down, the only ways to get supplies and reinforcements into Hue were via limited helicopter assets or by boat. The LCU was not molested, and it was offloaded by 1815. At 2015, a second LCU, loaded with a three-day supply of ammunition, arrived at the Hue LCU Ramp, and it was offloaded by 2230. Many other LCU sorties were scheduled for the days ahead.

At 1830, 2/5's three infantry companies stood down for the night and set in at the limit of the day's advances. When it halted, 2/5's most advanced element was little more than a block short of the 1st Marines' regimental objectives, the Prison and the Provincial Administrative Center.

If the true turning point in the battle for Hue had not been perceived on the evening of February 4, it was certainly evident on the evening of February 5 that, though still feisty, the NVA and VC in southern Hue were certainly on the defensive.

*

The first supply run to Hue using U.S. Navy landing craft arrived at the Hue LCU Ramp during the afternoon of February 5. Shown here, on a later run aboard a harbor utility craft, Marines and sailors scan the shore in search of snipers or heavy weapons that might attempt to impede the continuous flow of ammunition, food, and gear from Danang and other staging sites. *Official USMC Photo*

This Marine, a member of an M60 gun team, is ready to storm the next building. *Official USMC Photo*

February 6

At their nightly command conference following the February 5 action, Lieutenant Colonel Ernie Cheatham and his company commanders laid out a sort of holy mission for 2/5's February 6 advance. From the first full day of battle in Hue, the flagpole in front of the Thua Thien Provincial Administrative Center had shown the National Liberation Front battle colors. Cheatham and his officers agreed that the NLF flag must be pulled down on February 6 and that the Admin Center had to be liberated. All 2/5 needed to do to accomplish that mission—which coincided exactly with the 1st Marines regimental operations order—was battle its way across one more street and through one more narrow block of NVA-held buildings.

*

At 0425, positions manned by Captain Mike Downs' Fox/2/5, on the southeastern margin of the Hue Central Hospital complex, were struck by a volley of nine RPGs. One Marine was slightly injured. Fox/2/5 called for an immediate 81mm illumination mission and fired about a thousand small-arms rounds and six 3.5-inch rockets into the suspected source of the rocket fire. The NVA RPG teams were gone long before the cathartic return fire even began.

Emerging from the rubble of his last objective, this Marine is on the move, forward. *Official USMC Photo by Sergeant William L. Dickman*

All three companies of 2/5 jumped off at 0700 to clear the remainder of the Hospital complex and develop a line of departure facing the city block containing the Thua Thien Provincial Prison and the Admin Center. The NVA initially put up only light resistance, but 2/5 was slowed by the bred-in caution of Marines who had survived up to six days in

Marines from Fox/2/5 take a quick break from the rigors of urban combat. *Courtesy of Alexander Kandic*

By February 6, it was firm doctrine in 2/5 to place M60 machine guns in high overwatch positions while riflemen charged over open ground between buildings and blocks. *Official USMC Photos by Sergeant William L. Dickman*

Hue. They wanted to see how serious the NVA were about defending their ground before they committed themselves.

The Marines gnawed away at the NVA, and the NVA gnawed back. At 0734, Golf/2/5 Marines were engaged by snipers as they attacked the Hospital's main administration building through a billow of gas from four tear-gas grenades. Two NVA soldiers were cut down as they fled out a back door, and two Marines were wounded and evacuated.

At 0741, Hotel/2/5 Marines were fired on by an automatic weapon set in about 50 meters southwest of the company's front line. A Marine squad manning a base of fire responded with about a hundred M16 rounds, six M79 grenades, and two LAAWs, while another squad maneuvered toward the enemy position, delivered a volley of flanking fire, and attacked. The NVA fled, leaving two of their comrades dead on the ground.

Due to Golf/2/5's attack across Hotel/2/5's front on the afternoon of February 5, Hotel/2/5 was on the battalion's right flank when it

stepped off at 0820, February 6. The NVA facing Hotel/2/5 put up meager resistance against the opening move, and two more NVA soldiers were cut down in the open as they fled. Inside the first building Hotel/2/5 captured that day, the NVA left behind a large weapons cache.

As Hotel/2/5 awaited orders to jump off into the Admin Center, a truck carrying fresh replacements chugged up the street, passed right through the Hotel/2/5 line, and proceeded toward the company's objective. It was halfway there when the NVA fired on it. The driver immediately threw the vehicle into reverse and backed down to safety, but two of the Marines riding in the rear were left wounded in the street. It took patience, skill, and luck to recover both wounded Marines under NVA guns.

As Fox/2/5 maneuvered against a building on the 2/5 left flank at 0828, it was briefly held up by a pair of NVA who opened fire from the objective. The Marines responded with their M16s and two LAAWs, and then overran the position. Two more dead NVA were found.

The 2/5's February 6 advance on the Admin Center and Prison took a steady toll on veterans and replacements alike. Here, three Marines haul a wounded comrade to the rear through a break in a wall. *Official USMC Photo by Sergeant*

At 0905, elements of Golf/2/5 attacking through a very light screen of NVA skirmishers located and sent to the rear more than three hundred hospital patients and other civilian refugees. It appeared that the NVA were conceding the remainder of the Hospital complex to 2/5.

As soon as Hotel/2/5 reopened is attack upon the Admin Center at 0950, it was halted by intense fire all along its front. As the Marines engaged the NVA-fortified strongpoint with small-arms and machine-gun fire, two M48 tanks were called in, and a tripod-mounted 106mm recoilless rifle was manhandled to the front. Quickly, one of the tanks was struck by two RPGs, but it remained in action. Shortly, however, the NVA moved a 75mm recoilless rifle to a position on Hotel/2/5's right front, and the six rounds it fired subdued the attack. In their turn, the Marines called for 81mm mortar fire, and one hundred rounds were put out against various targets along Hotel/2/5's front.

As the Admin Center was being blanketed with heavy fire, Major John Salvati, 2/5's sanguinary executive officer, oversaw the emplacement of several tear-gas packs. Scores of 35mm gas pellets were fired, and then Hotel/2/5 Marines wearing gas masks launched a direct frontal assault into the objective. The area

around Hotel/2/5's February 6 objective was open to the breeze off the Perfume River, which worked to the advantage of the NVA defenders. Nevertheless, the Marines secured a fortified outbuilding inside the Admin Center—at a cost of five Marines wounded and evacuated. Twelve dead NVA were located in the strongpoint.

The Hospital complex, on the left flank of 2/5's zone, extended along the full city block southeast of and alongside the Prison. As Fox/2/5 continued its sweep through the Hospital, it entered the Antituberculosis Center and, in so doing, actually began to outflank the Prison's southeast wall.

At 1020, NVA resistance within the Antituberculosis Center suddenly stiffened. Apparently the NVA manning the Prison realized what Fox/2/5's possession of their southeastern flank would mean to them. The NVA in the Antituberculosis Center put up such a stubborn fight that Fox/2/5's stymied 2d Platoon had to call 81mm mortar and assorted artillery fire to bolster its own small-arms base of fire. As the company attack recommenced, an RPG struck a wall along which a Marine squad was dispersed. One Marine was mortally wounded.

Minutes later, from his position in a doorway facing toward the Prison, Captain Mike Downs could see Marines from Staff Sergeant Paul Tinson's 2d Platoon working their way up a side lane running at right angles to the Prison wall. One of the Marines got inside a hospital-ward building, but when Tinson and his platoon command group tried to follow, alert NVA on the Prison wall sealed the doorway with gunfire. Tinson backed off and went around to the other side of the building to look for another way in. Before he could, NVA manning another position opened fire. Tinson tried to backtrack, but the Marines behind him crowded him as they came around the blind corner from the rear of the building. In no time, the 2d Platoon command group got stalled in the open beside the hospital-ward building. Before Tinson could get

the stacked-up Marines turned around, NVA soldiers manning yet another overlook position chopped them all down.

Before Downs could react, NVA soldiers who could see him and his command group in the doorway of the small building opened fire on them. Downs was able to step out of the doorway in time, and he placed his back against the wall to his right. At the same moment, the captain's battalion radioman stepped back to the left. The company radioman had nowhere to go. He fell flat, half in and half out of the open doorway. A split second after the radioman fell, he started to flop spastically on the ground. He had been shot in the head three times.

Downs and two volunteers crossed the street under fire to try to rescue Staff Sergeant Tinson's fallen group. They ran up against a locked door, which they had to batter down. From inside the building, they could see the fallen Marines, but

there was no way to tell if any were alive. One of the volunteers crawled across the fire-swept alleyway to find out. Downs and the other volunteer fired their M16s at the Prison.

The news was grim. Tinson and another staff sergeant were dead, as were a radioman and a corpsman. Four other Marines had been wounded.

*

As it had on two previous mornings, 1/1 attempted to expand its holdings around the Jeanne d'Arc complex. Progress was slow, but gains were made against an NVA force that was clearly being reinforced from the south and southwest, through 1/1's open left flank. At 0900, Alpha/1/1's main body was engaged by NVA occupying a church half a block south of the Jeanne d'Arc complex and half a block east of the 1st Platoon's position inside the Jeanne d'Arc Student Center. The NVA fired an estimated two hundred small-arms rounds, and the

A Hotel/2/5 corpsman has set up an ad hoc first-aid and casualty clearing station behind a wall along the way to the Admin Center.
Official USMC Photo by Sergeant William L. Dickman

Marines responded with an estimated one thousand M16 and M60 rounds, ten 60mm mortar rounds, twenty 81mm mortar rounds, and two 106mm recoilless rifle rounds. Then the Alpha/1/1 Marines assaulted the church. Thirty dead NVA were recovered, a civilian man and woman were detained for questioning, and five rifles and one light machine gun were captured.

The NVA precipitously pulled out of the Jeanne d'Arc complex at 1100. As Marines from the main body of Alpha/1/1 fell into the vacuum created by the enemy's departure, they located seventeen dead NVA in the rubble of the western half of the once-beautiful Catholic girls' high school. As soon as the Jeanne d'Arc complex had been scoured, Alpha/1/1 and Bravo/1/1 reorganized and attacked to the southwest to catch up with 2/5.

At noon, Alpha/1/1 was caught on the move by a barrage of twenty 82mm mortar rounds. Eight Marines were wounded and evacuated, and another dozen casualties were treated and returned to the battle. The 1/1 attack continued at a much slower pace, but no further direct opposition was encountered until 1345. At that time, as Alpha/1/1 Marines eased along the southeastern edge of the Hospital complex, NVA soldiers directly to the south fired an estimated six hundred .51-caliber machine-gun rounds at them. The Marines responded with an estimated one thousand M16 and M60 rounds and twenty 60mm mortar

rounds. The enemy position was not attacked, however, and Alpha/1/1 pressed on to the southwest to close with 2/5. Two Marines were lightly wounded in the exchange, during which the NVA heavy machine gun was silenced or moved.

*

At 1305, approximately two dozen NVA soldiers who had been resisting Fox/2/5's ongoing attacks southeast of the Prison suddenly disengaged and withdrew toward the Prison itself. Fortunately, 2/5's 81mm mortars had already registered on the area, and fifty rounds were fired at the retreating NVA in a matter of seconds. Twenty-three of the fleeing NVA were killed in the open.

During the hour between 1300 and 1400, Golf/2/5 pressed the few remaining NVA out of the section of the Hospital complex in its zone. Thus, at 1405, Fox/2/5 was in secure positions on the southeastern flank of the Prison, Golf/2/5 was in line facing the Prison from the northeast, and Hotel/2/5 was in line on Golf/2/5's right, held up in its day-long bid to break into the Admin Center.

The Marines of 2/5 knew that the battalion's key moral objective was the Admin Center flagpole, on which the NVA had unfurled the NLF battle flag, but everyone assumed that the toughest nut yet taken on by 2/5 would be the Prison, which a reinforced Communist battalion had reduced against minimal opposition only after three days of hard fighting.

After nearly three hours of being softened up by mortars, artillery, and recoilless rifles, the NVA defending the Prison caved in. Aided by a heavy base of fire established by Fox/2/5, Golf/2/5 launched its final assault at 1405. The Prison's stout outer wall was breached at 1415, and in very little time the entire Prison complex was overrun at the cost of one Marine wounded and evacuated. Five ARVN soldiers and two prison officials were liberated. Altogether, thirty-six dead NVA were found, two NVA surrendered, and six men who could not explain their

presence were detained. Golf/2/5 Marines scouring the fortress policed up many weapons.

Hotel/2/5's progress through the Admin Center remained nil through the late morning and early afternoon. The NVA holed up in the rabbit warren of small office buildings put up a hell of a fight.

At 1425, while trying to jump-start its stalled assault, Hotel/2/5 was hit with yet another barrage of intense fire from the objective, including one RPG and several 75mm recoilless rifle rounds. The assaulting Marines once again stood down where they were and called for heavy preparatory fire, which mounted to one hundred 81mm mortar rounds and sixty 106mm recoilless rifle rounds. This barrage apparently broke the back of the defenses.

During the barrage, word came down from Captain Ron Christmas that Second Lieutenant Leo Myers' 1st Platoon was to kick in the door. Myers selected Private First Class Alan McDonald's squad to lead the way, and McDonald and his men drew straws to see who was going to be first in line. Private First Class Walter Kaczmarek picked first, and he drew the short straw.

A tear-gas launcher was fired, but Myers' platoon was called back because it went the wrong way as it stepped out into the thick, roiling clouds of tear gas. Another tear-gas pack was set up.

The second array of 35mm tear-gas pellets was launched, and the assault was on. There was noise coming from all directions, and the gas and the limited view through the gas mask lenses only made things worse.

A long board was thrown across the roll of concertina barbed wire the NVA had erected around the Admin Center, and Private First Class Kaczmarek led the way across. He had firm orders forbidding him to heave a fragmentation grenade through the objective's front door because the Marines had heard that the office

Lieutenant Leo Myers (at left, without gas mask) counts off his 1st Platoon of Hotel/2/5 as it charges single file into the tear-gas cloud covering the approach to the day's main objective, the Thua Thien Provincial Administrative Center. *Official USMC Photo by Sergeant William L.*

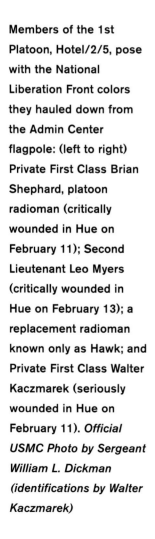

Members of the 1st Platoon, Hotel/2/5, pose with the National Liberation Front colors they hauled down from the Admin Center flagpole: (left to right) Private First Class Brian Shephard, platoon radioman (critically wounded in Hue on February 11); Second Lieutenant Leo Myers (critically wounded in Hue on February 13); a replacement radioman known only as Hawk; and Private First Class Walter Kaczmarek (seriously wounded in Hue on February 11). *Official USMC Photo by Sergeant William L. Dickman (identifications by Walter Kaczmarek)*

Private First Class Walter Kaczmarek (left) and Gunnery Sergeant Frank Thomas, both of Hotel/2/5, tie off the halyard after raising the Stars and Stripes in the Admin Center courtyard. *Official USMC Photo by Sergeant William L. Dickman*

building's walls were only plaster over lath, too thin to contain the blast.

Kaczmarek's view was restricted by the gas mask, so he fell over some rubble on the wide stairway fronting the entryway porch. When he had crawled to the top of the stairs, he emptied a full M16 magazine through the portal and scrambled into the foyer on his hands and knees. Most of the rest of Lieutenant Myers' platoon thundered into the lobby, right over Kaczmarek, and spread out.

NVA soldiers attempted to defend individual rooms and corridors on both floors, but the momentum of the attack carried the objective. Hotel/2/5 Marines recovered four NVA bodies.

As soon as Captain Christmas received word that the Admin Center was clear, he radioed Lieutenant Colonel Cheatham: "We have the building, sir. We're going to run up the American flag."

Strictly speaking, Christmas's plan to hoist the U.S. national colors was illegal. The building Hotel/2/5 had liberated was South Vietnamese government property. Indeed, American troops were forbidden to hoist the American flag on *any* liberated structure. But Christmas was adamant. When American troops, particularly Marines, are triumphant on a field of battle, the U.S. national colors, if available, are shown.

Christmas turned to Gunnery Sergeant Frank Thomas and said, "We've looked at that damn North Vietnamese flag all day, and now we are going to take it down. Let's go."

Thomas was prepared. He had put the word out that he was looking for a large American flag, but none was produced until two hard-bitten riflemen ran all the way back to MACV and pulled down—stole—the flag that was legally flying over that compound.

As the company commander and company gunny were laying on a proper flag ceremony, two uninvited guests turned up. The moment Private First Class Walter Kaczmarek laid eyes on the NLF flag, he decided that it was his if he could grab it. He talked his squad leader, Private First Class Alan McDonald, into helping him lower the enemy banner. The two had just reached the flagpole when Gunny Thomas appeared with the Stars and Stripes tucked into the front of his flak jacket. Thomas had no idea what Kaczmarek and McDonald were up to, but they were there, so he pressed them into service.

At 1603, with Captain Christmas, Lieutenant Myers, several other Marines, one ARVN interpreter, and a CBS camera crew looking on, Kaczmarek and McDonald struck the wet, limp NLF colors without fanfare, and Gunny Thomas cut them free from the halyard with his K-bar knife.

Then Old Glory was affixed to the halyard. As bullets popped and cracked nearby, and as wisps of tear gas floated around them, Kaczmarek and McDonald, who had a cigarette dangling from his lips, ran their nation's colors up the pole to stand in history beside American flags another generation of filthy, tired Marines had run up over Guadalcanal, Tarawa, Saipan, Iwo Jima, and Seoul. There was no time to call the onlookers to attention, no one remembered to salute, and the halyard became entangled for a few embarrassing moments, but there wasn't a dry eye in the crowd. Later, many of the onlookers sheepishly blamed their tears on the tear gas that was loose in their midst.

When Ernie Cheatham reported the fall of the Admin Center to Regiment, he told it like this: "Be advised we have taken the province headquarters. Somehow or other, an American flag is flying over there."

As soon as the deed was done, the CBS camera crew got a handful of the flag-raisers together to hold up the NLF banner and pose for pictures. All the time newsman Don Webster was giving his report to the camera, bullets popped and cracked in the background. As the correspondent wrapped up his report, Lieutenant Myers' Oklahoma drawl overcame all the other noise: "Hey, you finished? We want to get the hell out of here." There was still a battle to be won, and being in a static crowd inside Hue bothered the lieutenant and, when he brought the subject up, everyone else who was there.

The crowd around the flagpole dispersed in a flash as Lieutenant Myers and Gunny Thomas led their Marines back into the clearing operation.

*

Lieutenant Colonel Ernie Cheatham's victorious 2/5 set in at the limit of the day's advance at 1800. That evening, Alpha/1/1 caught up and relieved Fox/2/5 in the Antituberculosis Center. Then, for the first time since it had entered Hue, Fox/2/5 went into reserve.

In four days of vicious combat, 2/5 had broken the backs of two and possibly three NVA infantry battalions and an unknown number of VC units. Thereafter, though the Communist troops fought on against 2/5 and 1/1 for nearly three more weeks, the 4th NVA Regiment ceased to be a strategically relevant factor in the battle for Hue.

In due course, as seen here, the Stars and Stripes was replaced with the Republic of Vietnam national colors. The Marines who took the Admin Center charged through tear gas and heavy fire, through the gate, past the flagpole, up the steps, and through the main entrance.
Official USMC Photo

Chapter 7

SCENES FROM THE SOUTH SIDE

February 7–March 8, 1968

At 0530, February 7, NVA sappers who apparently had worked through the night blew the two center spans of the Nguyen Hoang Bridge into the Perfume River. For the moment, the gesture was rather pointless, as there was no American or ARVN effort that even looked like it might be aimed at the bridge. Indeed, the demolition of the bridge and the resulting isolation of the 6th NVA Regiment from the 4th NVA Regiment suggested that the turning point in Hue had been acknowledged by the NVA commanders. There was no longer any point to the Communist occupation of Hue, but three weeks of bloody street fighting remained to be endured.

*

All of Hue stank of rotting corpses tinged with tear gas and smoke from hundreds of untended fires. Thousands of dogs and barnyard animals were loose in the streets, gorging themselves on the hundreds and thousands of dead animals and people. Desperate for food and water, thousands of defenseless civilians risked life and limb to reach Marine or ARVN lines, where they knew they would be fed and where they could have their wounds treated.

In the course of a few days, the Hue University complex, liberated on February 2, became an overcrowded refugee relief center. By the late morning of February 7, five thousand Vietnamese civilians were being cared for there. Though all the supplies the Marines consumed had to be lifted to Hue aboard helicopters or landing craft, a huge stockpile of foodstuffs and other disaster-relief items maintained by the Government of Vietnam in Hue was more than adequate to meet their basic needs.

*

The Marines' early morning advance on February 7 fell into a vacuum. The NVA had withdrawn from 2/5's and 1/1's front, leaving the bodies of their dead, odd lots of military gear, and many untended weapons. By noon, the Marines had advanced through buildings and compounds comprising an area two full city

Hue by firelight.

Official USMC Photo

An overhead view of the blown bridge. *Official USMC Photo*

blocks wide and two full city blocks deep—all without encountering more than the odd sniper. As each major structure was scoured by the infantry companies, the 2/5 and 1/1 intelligence analysts and scouts combed the area for booty and bodies from which documents and other intelligence matter could be retrieved. In the course of the morning, Marine infantry units and intelligence teams turned up the battlefield graves of sixty-two NVA or VC soldiers and cataloged the retrieval of scores of weapons.

At 1245, Golf/2/5 Marines scouring the Directorate of Social Welfare compound, hard by the Phu Cam Canal, discovered the bodies of three Caucasian males who appeared to be Americans. The corpses were checked by an intelligence team and evacuated to MACV.

The first significant resistance to the February 7 Marine sweep came at 1530, as

A Marine patrol moves up Le Loi Street. February 7. *Official USMC Photo by Sergeant William L. Dickman*

Golf/2/5 closed on the Le Lai Military Camp, about 150 meters due south of the Prison and a short block north of the Phu Cam Canal. In addition to armed NVA infantrymen holed up in buildings, the Marines were hit by four 60mm mortar rounds. As Golf/2/5 deployed to attack the enemy position, an 81mm preparatory fire mission was called. The attack, which jumped off at 1600, overran the NVA strongpoint and produced eleven more NVA corpses. Nevertheless, the bulk of the military camp remained in enemy hands.

At 1746, elements of Hotel/2/5 were struck by four 82mm mortar rounds as they searched through a large building two blocks southwest of the Prison. Ten Marines were wounded. An immediate counter-mortar mission fired by 2/5's 81mm mortars either silenced the NVA mortar or forced it to displace.

The only Marine killed in Hue on February 7 was First Lieutenant Gordon Matthews, the Bravo/1/1 commander. Relatively few were wounded. In the course of the day, 2/5 and 1/1 found that the NVA had abandoned, virtually

Fleeing Communist troops are gunned down whenever they can be seen. Fox/2/5 sector. *Courtesy of Alexander Kandic*

Wary Fox/2/5 Marines pause for a breather along the north bank of the Phu Cam Canal. February 8. *Courtesy of Alexander Kandic*

without a fight, the entire triangular area between the Perfume River, the Phu Cam Canal, and a north–south line from the Prison to the canal. NVA stragglers or snipers still infested the area, but it was as good as liberated.

*

February 8 was another pretty easy day for the Marines, though the NVA kicked it off with a 0530 wake-up call at MACV that consisted of ten 122mm rockets launched from

sites well to the south of the city. A Marine artillery battery near Nam Hoa fired its six 105mm howitzers at the telltale rocket-ignition flashes. The rocket fire stopped, but no results could be observed.

At 0547, Marines from Alpha/1/1 spotted a small NVA force moving into a building a block south of the Jeanne d'Arc Student Center. M16 and M60 fire dispersed the NVA.

The almost persistent collection of odd lots of NVA bodies, weapons, ammunition, and equipment conveyed to the Marines a loss of discipline and esprit among the NVA battalions. It was almost unheard of for NVA units to leave their dead or very much gear on a battlefield. As the body count and small-arms and equipment caches added up, it became evident that the 4th NVA Regiment was having discipline and morale problems, which were taken to mean command and control problems. Of the small number of prisoners taken, a large proportion were officers and senior sergeants, a factor of great significance.

Beginning at 0700, Hotel/2/5 and Fox/2/5 opened an attack to the south to close on the

Led by a weary-looking 3.5-inch-rocket gunner, an Alpha/1/1 squad moves through the wreckage of a building to avoid the shooting gallery on the street. February 8. *Official USMC Photo*

Phu Cam Canal. Once at the canal, 2/5 was to wheel to the east and attack in that direction as far as Highway 1.

At 0705, on the battalion's right, Hotel/2/5 came under heavy machine-gun fire from a building on its left flank. A vigorous response with small arms and M79 grenades, bolstered by an 81mm mortar barrage, forced the NVA from their position. Hotel/2/5 overran the objective.

At 0710, while attacking on Hotel/2/5's left (east) flank, Fox/2/5 ran into sniper fire along its front. The enemy position was overcome with small-arms fire at the cost of two Marines wounded, two NVA killed, and one NVA soldier taken prisoner.

At 0944, Hotel/2/5 attacked the Le Lai Military Camp, from which Golf/2/5 had had to withdraw the previous evening. The camp

An Alpha/1/1 fire team prepares to move out from a church in southern Hue.
February 9. *Official USMC Photo by Sergeant Bruce Atwell*

A 1/1 106mm recoilless rifle is manhandled to the front. February 9.
Official USMC Photo by Sergeant Bruce Atwell

February 9. *Official USMC Photo by Sergeant Bruce Atwell*

was overrun again at around 1000, this time at the cost of one Marine killed, one Marine wounded, and one NVA soldier killed. Marines quickly stumbled on the ARVN's main armory in Hue. Apparently the store of weapons and munitions had not been molested by the NVA, for, in addition to a huge stockpile of ammunition and military equipment, the Marines inventoried 1,500 rifles, carbines, and submachine guns, one hundred U.S.-made .30-caliber light machine guns, four 57mm recoilless rifles, fifteen M113 armored personnel carriers, and eight M41 light tanks.

*

At 1000, two platoons of Bravo/1/1 were sweeping along Highway 1 from the northwest in the direction of the An Cuu Bridge when they were was accosted by NVA holed up in the Thua Thien Province Police Bureau, a walled compound halfway across the canefield

Before he steps from cover, this Marine confers with the photographer, who has a better view of what lies ahead. February 10. *Official USMC Photo by Lance Corporal R. J. Smith*

causeway. The Marines returned the fire with even stronger fire and maneuvered into the compound, where they found three dead NVA and an armory containing 2.5 tons of assorted arms and munitions.

*

While the infantry companies were active to the east, the engineer platoon attached to 2/5 was put to work preparing the westernmost

A large convoy from Phu Bai was turned back at the Phu Cam Canal when engineers determined they could not get the An Cuu Bridge rebuilt before nightfall. February 10. *Courtesy of Dr. Jerome Nadolski*

bridge across the Phu Cam Canal for demolition. At 1005, the engineers were fired on by NVA snipers south of the canal. Three engineers who were wounded could not be evacuated until Marine M48 tanks arrived to cover the rescue

Captives await a helicopter ride to Phu Bai. February 10. *Official USMC Photo by First Lieutenant B. T. Cummins*

A 106mm recoilless rifle team and infantry escorts search for a target. February 11. *Official USMC Photo by Lance Corporal R. J. Smith*

This Communist soldier died as he tangled with superior Marine firepower. February 12. *Official USMC Photo*

Hotel/2/5 scours a shell-blasted house. Note the cathedral spire at left. *Official USMC Photo by Sergeant William L. Dickman*

effort with 90mm smoke rounds and fire on the enemy position with their .50- and .30-caliber machine guns.

The notion of Marines demolishing a bridge within a city they were liberating in the course of a battle they were winning bears some explanation. The Marine commanders felt that a counterattack based south of the Phu Cam Canal might be in the offing, and that it was easier to demolish a bridge than to use limited troops to develop a strongpoint around it. The bridge in question—the westernmost of six that spanned the canal—was not militarily vital to the Marines; the reason for blowing it or any other bridge across the Phu Cam Canal was to deny the enemy approach routes from the south into the newly liberated provincial seat. Higher headquarters felt that there were adequate engineering assets and bridging materials deployed in northern I Corps to assure that all the bridges across the canal could be replaced easily whenever they needed to be.

Plans were afoot to mount the 1st Marine Bridge Company out of Phu Bai the next day to replace the NVA-demolished An Cuu Bridge across the other end of the Phu Cam Canal. The bridge company, which was to be escorted by a platoon of the real Bravo/1/1 and all available replacements bound for 2/5, was to be met at the bridge site by Alpha/1/1 and the main body of the provisional Bravo/1/1.

Sparring with NVA rear-guard detachments and stragglers consumed most of the afternoon of February 8. More NVA bodies, weapons, and gear fell into Marine hands.

At 1315, Golf/2/5 Marines entered the U.S. consul general's residence, on Ly Thuong Kiet Street, right across from the cathedral, and only half a block west of the canefield that stretched out on both sides of the Highway 1 causeway. Reaching the consular quarters brought Captain Chuck Meadows and the Golf/2/5 survivors virtually full circle, for the first shots fired at them in the battle for Hue had been put out by an NVA machine gun set in near the cathedral.

As soon as the Marines entered the consul general's residence, they turned up evidence that the compound had been used by the NVA as a field dispensary. Bloody bandages and other medical waste, plus abandoned medical supplies abounded. In short order, twenty hastily constructed graves

Hotel/2/5 Marines jog across a bridge spanning the Phu Cam Canal. February 12. *Official USMC Photo by Lance Corporal R. J. Smith*

were discovered, and a total of twenty-five dead NVA soldiers were exhumed.

Outside of the battle zone on February 8, several LCUs arrived at the Hue LCU Ramp, chock full of ammunition and other useful gear

Communist mortar rounds slam into an area in southern Hue occupied by Hotel/2/5. The Communists were able to resist Marine advances throughout Hue with rockets and mortars. *Official USMC Photo by Sergeant William L. Dickman*

On February 13, the Hotel/2/5 command group, Hotel/2/5's 1st Platoon, and part of Fox/2/5 were struck by a devastating mortar barrage. Here, the ambulatory wounded wait at the Hue LCU Ramp for a seaborne lift to Danang. February 14. *Courtesy of Richard Carter (standing on the right)*

A Marine tank stands off from its target in the Hotel/2/5 zone and pounds an objective with 90mm rounds. Note the seven shell casings beside the M48. *Official USMC Photo by Sergeant William L. Dickman*

and equipment. The last LCU to leave the ramp that afternoon was fired on heavily by small arms and mortars, but it ran the gauntlet to the South China Sea without damage. The LCU lifts were extremely important in that the continuously foul weather was rendering helicopter resupply efforts fairly moot.

*

On February 9, NVA gunners started the day by terrorizing the MACV Compound with six 60mm mortar rounds. The 1st Marines command post, which was inside the compound, arranged for counter-battery missions against the area southeast of the city in which muzzle flashes had been observed. Against the one or two NVA light mortars, the Marines fired ten 81mm mortar rounds and, from Phu Bai, eight 155mm rounds. Damage and casualties could not be assessed.

The task of securing the An Cuu Bridge site was given to 1/1, which was to attack from the north, down the northeastern side of the canefield, from the vicinity of Tu Do Stadium. Cheatham's 2/5 was to secure the northern side of the Phu Cam Canal all the way from the Perfume River to a battalion boundary line set just east of the An Cuu Bridge.

Alpha/1/1 ran into opposition only after clearing two city blocks, including Tu Do Stadium, without firing a shot. At 0820, as the company point pushed east from the Stadium, four Marines on the point were wounded as they crossed a street. In the ensuing exchange, it took three 90mm rounds fired by the attached M48 tank to get Alpha/1/1 across the street. At 0900 the NVA hit the tank with seven 57mm recoilless rifle rounds. The tank was set afire and abandoned on the spot by its crew, three of whom were burned and needed to be evacuated.

It is not surprising that 1/1 encountered such strong opposition in its new zone. Apparently the Marine demibattalion was facing the still-intact main body of the 804th NVA Battalion, which had not been seriously engaged

The southern Hue marketplace was leveled in the fighting. February 14. *Official USMC Photo*

Fox/2/5 Marines question a civilian. February 16. *Official USMC Photo*

or harmed by the Marine clearing operation for all of the preceding week.

Shortly after the damaged M48 tank was towed away, an ARVN major who had been home for Tet leave entered the Alpha/1/1 lines after leaving his house for the first time since January 31. The ARVN officer pinpointed his house on Second Lieutenant Ray Smith's map and told Smith that the building next door was the site of an NVA battalion command post—

presumably the 804th NVA Battalion. Before being escorted to MACV, the ARVN major said that a Chinese advisor was stationed with the NVA command group. Lieutenant Smith passed these tidbits up the chain of command and requested permission to level the area around the enemy command post with some really serious artillery fire. Permission was conditionally granted—if higher headquarters agreed.

At 1020, while pulling out of the line of the anticipated friendly fire, Alpha/1/1 was struck by an estimated two hundred small-arms rounds and three RPGs. The Marines returned fire with

This gas station in southern Hue has been virtually destroyed in the fighting. *Official USMC Photo*

A Fox/2/5 M60 team (bottom left corner) has staked out this gas station before riflemen move in to check it out. *Courtesy of Alexander Kandic*

Before moving on the suspected hideout of an NVA sniper, a Fox/2/5 squad leader (the bareheaded Marine) confers with his troops. Then a grenadier opens the action when he fires his M79. February 18. *Official USMC Photos*

M16s, M60s, and six LAAWs. Three Marines were wounded and evacuated in the exchange, and two of eight NVA soldiers who sprinted into an open area were killed by a direct hit from one of the LAAWs.

At 1325, Bravo/1/1 was struck by yet another group of NVA. At the outset of the exchange, an accompanying army M55 quad-.50 truck was rendered inoperable by an RPG. At the cost of one Marine wounded, the enemy strongpoint was silenced by a cloud of fire. Five minutes after the M55 was damaged, the main body of Alpha/1/1 was struck by ten 60mm mortar rounds fired from north of Tu Do Stadium. By then, higher headquarters had come back with permission for Lieutenant Smith to fire all available artillery at the 804th NVA Battalion command post.

In the largest artillery barrage to strike Hue to date, an artillery forward observer directed a total of about two hundred fifty 8-inch howitzer rounds, nearly five hundred 155mm gun rounds, and all the 81mm mortar rounds the 1/1 81mm Mortar Platoon could spare against the 804th NVA Battalion's zone south and east of the Tu Do Stadium. For all the artillery fire, it was painfully obvious by the middle of the afternoon that 1/1 was not going to be able to close on the An Cuu Bridge from the north that day. At 1515, the battalion attack was canceled and Lieutenant Colonel Gravel's two thin infantry companies were ordered to consolidate a night defensive position at the limit of their advances. At 1515, the main body of Bravo/1/1 was harassed by NVA snipers, who fired sixty rounds and wounded three Marines. The Marines responded, as usual, with M16 and M60 fire, this time bolstered with an 81mm mortar fire mission, but results could not be determined.

Five more Bravo/1/1 Marines were wounded during another exchange, at 1600, and yet another exchange, at 1745, resulted in two Marines killed. A 105mm howitzer mission was placed on the source of the enemy fire, but that had no lasting effect.

*

During a well-deserved break, Fox/2/5 Marines light up, gab, and catch a catnap. February 18. *Official USMC Photos courtesy of Alexander*

At 0828, February 9, shortly after moving without opposition into the sprawling Phu Cam Cathedral complex, Captain Chuck Meadows' Golf/2/5 turned up a cache of six hundred tons of rice and one ARVN M41 tank. After liberating hundreds of civilian refugees from the cathedral and adjacent buildings, Golf/2/5 continued to apply pressure on the NVA manning positions in and around the canefield southwest of Highway 1. At 1005, in Golf/2/5's only action of the morning, both army M42 Dusters attached to the Marine company were disabled when their gas tanks were holed by NVA fire. Fortunately, neither Duster burned, and both were towed to the rear for repairs. One Marine was killed and two Marines were wounded in the exchange.

At 1820, as engineers accompanying Golf/2/5 placed charges to drop the first bridge to the west of the An Cuu Bridge into the Phu Cam Canal, NVA to the south put out an intense volley of small-arms and automatic-weapons

Hotel/2/5 riflemen converge outside a walled compound to engage Communist troops holed up in a house. *Official USMC Photo by Sergeant William L. Dickman*

A Golf/2/5 M60 team mans a makeshift bunker with a clear view of one of the bridges across the Phu Cam Canal. February 20. *Official USMC Photo*

Almost as soon as the center spans of the Nguyen Hoang Bridge were blown on February 7, civilians fleeing the fighting in and around the Citadel resorted to travel to the southern bank via sampan. Soon, Vietnamese engineers began work on a walkway to connect the dropped spans, and that reopened a floodgate of refugees from the northern bank. Once on the southern side of the river, they became part of a refugee community seventy thousand strong that turned to the government for protection instead of revolting against it, as expected by the Communists. *Official USMC Photo by First Lieutenant B. T. Cummins*

fire. This fire was quelled and the bridge was blown, but one Golf/2/5 Marine was killed and two others were wounded. Altogether, throughout the day, in addition to recovering the rice and the ARVN tank, Golf/2/5 accounted for seventeen NVA killed. Two Golf/2/5 Marines were killed on February 9, and five were wounded.

At 1051, as the 3d Platoon of Captain Ron Christmas's Hotel/2/5 moved east alongside the Phu Cam Canal, it was struck from south of the canal by small-arms fire. One Marine was killed. At 1220, a routine search turned up three Vietnamese men clad in civilian clothes and carrying a carbine, a submachine gun, and an RPG round. At 1305 the company apprehended eight more civilian-garbed Vietnamese men who were monitoring a Marine artillery fire net on a transistor radio. At 1720, after being prevented by NVA fire from demolishing the second Phu Cam Bridge east of the An Cuu Bridge, Hotel/2/5 called in an 8-inch howitzer mission to drop the span. When the initial rounds fell astride the target, they produced two large secondary explosions on the southern side of the canal. A moment later, eight enemy soldiers were shot to death in the open as they fled from a strongpoint beside the bridge. No Marines were even scratched during the incident.

Altogether, on February 9, 2/5 completed the liberation of all but the eastern tip of the triangular area bordered by the Perfume River, the Phu Cam Canal, and Highway 1. Much of the newly liberated area still had to be scoured more carefully, but it was evident that the 4th NVA Regiment had been ejected from Hue's modern central area. The inability of 1/1 to breast the defensive sector held by the remnants of the 804th NVA Battalion necessitated a one-day delay in the deployment of the 1st Marine Bridge Company at the as-yet unsecured An Cuu Bridge site.

*

Throughout February 10, 2/5 cleared NVA stragglers and collected their discarded weapons and equipment from the built-up areas north of the Phu Cam Canal. Three 2/5 Marines were wounded all day in exchange for nine confirmed kills.

In the 1/1 zone, the attack toward the An Cuu Bridge was canceled. Instead, Alpha/1/1 and Bravo/1/1 were put to work clearing the 804th NVA Battalion out of the neighborhoods to the east and southeast of Tu Do Stadium.

An Alpha/1/1 squad patrols a neighborhood near the Phu Cam Canal. February 29. *Official USMC Photo by Lance Corporal D. M. Messenger*

In the only significant action of the day undertaken by 1/1, Alpha/1/1 fired tear gas and threw in a dawn attack against the reported site of the 804th NVA Battalion command post. Marines searching through the rubble left in the wake of the previous afternoon's massive artillery strike noted that the designated building had a command post–like setup, complete with tattered NVA battle flags. Several bodies were exhumed from the rubble, but large pools of congealing blood and numerous blood trails and drag marks indicated that many dead and wounded had been withdrawn during the night.

As in the 2/5 zone, contacts through the remainder of the day were limited and light, casualties were light, and results were limited. The 804th NVA Battalion didn't quite give the area up, but it did not put up much of a fight.

As the fighting petered out, Marines were detailed to assist refugees to relocation centers in southern Hue. *Official USMC Photo by Lance Corporal R. J. Smith*

Here, Marines and ARVN soldiers hand out food to Hue refugees who will soon be taken to shelters outside the city. *Official USMC Photo*

At 1235, February 10, the delayed bridge convoy, guarded by a platoon of the real Bravo/1/1 and including 150 replacements bound for 2/5, was ordered out of Phu Bai. When it arrived safely and without incident at the An Cuu Bridge site, the Marine engineers discovered that the condition of the span was far worse than had been communicated or anticipated, and that adequate bridging materials had not been brought along. The 1st Marine Bridge Company and a serial of trucks laden with supplies bound for 1/1 and 2/5 returned to Phu Bai, but all of the nearly two hundred infantrymen crossed the shattered span on foot and walked to MACV. The Bravo/1/1 platoon was turned over to 1/1, and

the replacements were sent to 2/5. A number of the 2/5 replacements were among the first Marines to be returned to the battalion following earlier injury and evacuation in Hue.

*

For all practical purposes, the mission assigned to the 1st Marines by Task Force X-Ray on February 3 had been accomplished by the end of the day on February 10. The entire heart of modern Hue bounded by Highway 1, the Perfume River, and the Phu Cam Canal was free of organized NVA or VC opposition. Moreover, the 804th NVA Battalion's resistance in the built-up area east of Highway 1 and south of the Perfume appeared to be on the verge of collapse. In the days ahead, 1/1 continued to clear the

enemy from its zone around Tu Do Stadium while, in the absence of firm orders from above, Lieutenant Colonel Ernie Cheatham, on his own authority, eased elements of 2/5 into the built-up areas south of the Phu Cam Canal to see if they were strongly held. Many 1/1 and 2/5

Marines would be wounded or killed in the "routine" clearing operations that ensued into early March. Among them, on February 13, was Hotel/2/5's Captain Ron Christmas, whose severe leg injuries were the result of a mortar barrage.

Chapter 8

BATTLES FOR THE CITADEL

February 1–9, 1968

As soon as the defense within the 1st ARVN Division compound, in the northern corner of the Citadel of Hue, was stabilized on the morning of January 31, Brigadier General Ngo Quang Truong sought reinforcements from I ARVN Corps. Initially this came in the form of the three-hundred-man 2d ARVN Airborne Battalion, which was in a temporary bivouac north of the city. As soon as the lead airborne company reached the northern built-up area, it was stopped by a deeply entrenched NVA battalion.

Also made available to Truong were the 1st ARVN Airborne Battle Group headquarters, the 7th ARVN Airborne Battalion, and a troop of the 7th Armored Cavalry Battalion. These hardened units were at a former French army camp known as PK 17 (because it was 17 kilometers north of Hue, at Post Kilometer 17).

The command post of the 3d ARVN Regiment, an organic part of the 1st ARVN Division, was also at PK 17, and the regiment's four battalions held various camps around the city.

During the day, all four battalions made contact with Communist forces in somewhat coordinated moves toward the Citadel.

On the Communist side on January 31, the 5th NVA Regiment was able to erect a screen around the northwestern quadrant of the city and block Highway 1 between the Citadel and PK 17, but it was stretched thin. Inside the Citadel, the 6th NVA Regiment harassed the 1st ARVN Division command compound and scoured several areas, but it gained no new ground against ARVN forces after Truong conceded Tay Loc Airfield.

*

At 0800 hours on February 1, the 1st ARVN Airborne Battle Group headquarters, its 2d and 7th ARVN Airborne battalions, and an armored cavalry troop breached the 6th NVA Regiment defenses with the help of ARVN 105mm howitzers based at PK 17 and ran all the way into the 1st ARVN Division command compound. The battalions of the 3d ARVN

The northern corner of the Citadel of Hue, site of (1) the 1st ARVN Division command compound and (2) Tay Loc Airfield. *Official USMC Photo*

ARVN airborne soldiers are airlifted aboard Marine Medium Helicopter Squadron 346 CH-46 helicopters.
Official USMC Photo

Regiment continued to attack toward the Citadel with limited but nonetheless positive results. Indeed, at 1500, the 1st Battalion, 3d ARVN Regiment, fought its way into the division command compound after crossing the Perfume River aboard motorized junks.

During the day, General Truong heard that on February 2 the 9th ARVN Airborne Battalion was to be flown from Saigon to PK 17 and that U.S. Marine helicopters would lift the 4th Battalion, 2d ARVN Regiment, directly into the command compound.

*

On the morning of February 2, as the 9th ARVN Airborne Battalion was being helilifted directly into the 1st ARVN Division command compound, the division's elite Black Panther (Hoc Bao) Company led an attack force that included the 2d and 7th ARVN Airborne battalions to retake Tay Loc Airfield and the ordnance compound.

As the day progressed, the 4th Battalion, 2d ARVN Regiment, and a company of the 3d Battalion, 1st ARVN Regiment, were also lifted into the Citadel command compound. These additions probably placed Truong's fighting force at superior numerical advantage over the Communist force in and right around the Citadel.

*

On the downside, the 1st ARVN Engineer Battalion came under strong attack south of the city on February 3. As well, the large but largely untrained 4th Battalion, 3d ARVN Regiment, became surrounded in a battle east of MACV as it attempted to maneuver from its training camp. Its prospects appeared rather grim. Further, the 2d and 3d battalions, 3d ARVN Regiment, were unable to make progress toward the Citadel and, indeed, both were pinned against the fortress's southern corner.

On balance, however, the 1st ARVN Division was doing well inside the Citadel, where the 6th NVA Regiment definitely went over to the defensive. Nevertheless, the Communist forces facing Truong's burgeoning command had a lot of fight in them.

*

General Truong expanded his offensive within the Citadel on February 4. One infantry battalion attacked along the northwestern wall and seized the An Hoa Gate, and another

infantry battalion fought to about halfway down the northeastern wall.

The ARVN battalions battling toward the Citadel made little progress, but they did keep NVA and VC battalions engaged in denying them access to the fortress. On the other hand, the 4th Battalion, 3d ARVN Regiment, fought its way to MACV. The unit had started out with about 700 effectives, mostly recruits, but it mustered only 170 effectives when it paused at MACV to catch its breath.

*

Farther out from Hue, the Communist high command for the conquest of Quang Tri and Thua Thien provinces, including Hue, had set up a headquarters at a village just off Highway 1 midway between the Citadel and PK 17. A battalion of the U.S. 1st Cavalry Division, which was in the process of redeploying into northern I Corps just as Tet got under way, was ordered out of PK 17 on February 3, and in due course it tangled with powerful elements of the 5th NVA Regiment that were providing security for the regional high command. The Cav battalion was out of its element—it had dismounted from its helicopters and had never before fought in the area—and thus it was ordered to withdraw following a bloody two-day stalemate almost within sight of the Communist command post.

ARVN troops have just cleared this block of shops inside the Citadel. *Colonel Chuck Meadows Collection*

These well-equipped ARVN troops have more than the usual fire power in the M41 light tank that has joined them in this curbside firefight. *Official USMC Photo*

Large bombs strike buildings between the northern bank of the Perfume River and the southeastern Citadel wall. *Official USMC Photo*

In due course, very powerful elements of the 1st Cavalry and 101st Airborne divisions would be engaged in sealing Hue from outside the 5th NVA Regiment cordon, and then in attacking toward the city. For now, however, the appearance of the Cav battalion between Hue and PK 17 gave the Communists a great deal of concern and thus tied down units needed elsewhere.

*

On February 5, the 1st ARVN Airborne Task Force (as it became known after the addition of the 9th ARVN Airborne Battalion) took over the attack along the Citadel's northeastern wall, and an ARVN infantry battalion attacked abreast the airborne units, thus widening the 1st ARVN Division holdings in that direction. The 4th Battalion, 3d ARVN Regiment, was moved from MACV, via the Hue LCU Ramp, to the northern bank. It gallantly made seven successive bids to secure the Thuong Tu Gate into the Citadel, but it finally had to back off down Highway 1 to join with its regiment's embattled 2d and 3d battalions along the outer southwestern wall.

*

Despite heavy sparring, the situation on the northern bank remained unchanged on February 6. But late in the morning of February 7, a large Communist force assaulted the battered 4th Battalion, 3d ARVN Regiment, outside the Chanh Tay Gate. The battalion barely saved itself during a last-ditch stand.

In the largest air strike to date over Hue, Vietnam Air Force A-1 Skyraider single-engine attack bombers dropped twenty-four 500-pound bombs on NVA positions along the Citadel's outer southeastern wall. Many NVA were killed, but the Communist defenses remained intact.

ARVN units mounting attacks on February 7 were unable to make measurable gains. Indeed, ARVN units in and around the

ARVN medics treat a woman wounded in the fighting in the Citadel. *Texas Tech Virtual Vietnam Archive/Douglas Pike Photo Collection*

Citadel had been fought to a complete standstill. Even though they were spirited troops with good leadership and modern equipment, the small ARVN battalions wielded nothing resembling the sheer firepower that even American infantry companies possessed. They were not going to be driven back by the Communist units they faced, but neither could they drive through them.

Chapter 9

REINFORCING THE CITADEL

February 10–12, 1968

On February 10, ARVN General Headquarters informed Brigadier General Ngo Quang Truong that it wanted to withdraw all airborne units from Hue to reconstitute the ARVN strategic reserve. Truong pointed out that he might lose the Citadel in that case, so the South Vietnamese Joint General Staff offered two reinforced Vietnam Marine Corps (VNMC) battalions. Truong accepted, and then MACV in Saigon offered a fresh U.S. Marine infantry battalion for duty in the Citadel.

The U.S. Marine battalion selected was Major Robert Thompson's 1st Battalion, 5th Marines, which on February 10 was in action to the hilt in Hai Van Pass, near Phu Loc. During the morning, Alpha/1/5 was detached and ordered to Phu Bai, and then on to Hue. Later, two platoons of Bravo/1/5 were ordered to Phu Bai, and then the rest of the battalion was put on notice for the move. At midnight, 1/5 passed to the control of 5th Marines, at which moment the regimental command post

ordered Bob Thompson to disengage immediately and move his troops to Phu Bai posthaste. The battalion had to withdraw from a battle in the dead of night under cover of an extremely cold rainstorm.

Thompson and the forward and rear elements of the battalion command group reached Phu Bai by 0930, February 11. The battalion commander and his staff took on a hazy briefing at the Task Force X-Ray command post that imparted no useful information. Experienced Hue hands who happened to be at Phu Bai told Thompson to unpack his battalion's 3.5-inch rocket launchers as well as informally briefed him on what they had learned about urban warfare.

At 1045, Captain Fernandez Jennings' Bravo/1/5 left Phu Bai aboard four Marine helicopters. One pilot was wounded while approaching Hue, and he aborted to Phu Bai with an infantry platoon aboard. The rest of Bravo/1/5 landed inside the 1st ARVN Division command compound without further incident.

Grim-faced and battle-weary, this platoon of 1/5 crosses the Perfume River aboard an LCU crammed alongside trucks laden with 105mm ammunition on its way to South Vietnamese units. *Official USMC Photo*

Major Bob Thompson, 1/5's combative and highly competent commanding officer, was given almost no information or advice from higher headquarters before he arrived in the Citadel of Hue on February 12. As had been the case with 1/1 and 2/5, Thompson and 1/5 had to face a steep learning curve on the job. *Courtesy of Donald Young*

The aborted Bravo/1/5 platoon left Phu Bai as road escort for the battalion forward command group, and both reached the MACV Compound at 1800 hours after crossing a jury-rigged footbridge at the site of the shattered An Cuu Bridge.

Throughout February 12, the main body of 1/5 moved into Hue, where Delta/1/5 was attached to 2/5. The rest of the battalion crossed the Perfume aboard LCUs that put them ashore at a secure quay beside the ARVN-held northern corner of the Citadel. The battalion was reinforced by a platoon of five 1st Tank Battalion M48 gun tanks that made the trip from Danang aboard LCUs. At 2015, Thompson contacted the 1st Marines command post with the news that he would jump off into the attack at 0800, February 13, unless otherwise directed. He also mentioned that there was neither sign nor word of the two promised VNMC battalions.

The VNMC Battle Group Alpha headquarters was indeed closing on Hue with the 1st and 5th VNMC battalions and a six-gun 105mm howitzer battery, but its commander was determined to take all his units in together, while U.S. Marine commanders wanted to

A truck carrying Vietnamese marines from the An Cuu footbridge to the Hue LCU Ramp passes a vehicle carrying a Fox/2/5 patrol. *Courtesy of Alexander Kandic*

commit them piecemeal as they reached Hue via the An Cuu footbridge. It also required a lot of bickering before the VNMC troops were able to draw needed gear—including winter jackets—from U.S. Marine stocks at Phu Bai. In the end, Battle Group Alpha shoved off intact by truck from Phu Bai, crossed the An Cuu footbridge, marched to the Hue LCU Ramp, loaded aboard landing craft, and disembarked at the quay beside the northern corner of the Citadel. By the late evening of February 12, the battle group commander reported his units ready to commence action in the morning.

For the final attack to liberate the Citadel of Hue, 1/5 was to relieve the 1st ARVN Airborne Task Force in place about halfway along the northeastern Citadel wall, then attack toward the eastern corner with its left flank at the wall. The main body of the 3d ARVN Regiment would continue to operate in the vicinity of the Citadel's western corner, and VNMC Battle Group Alpha would be employed as needed, probably beginning with the relief of exhausted 1st ARVN Division units fighting near Tay Loc Airfield and the Chanh Tay Gate. American senior officers decided that 1st Marines—rather than 1st ARVN Division—would control 1/5. This was an insult to the extremely competent and combative Truong, but he showed no sign of taking offense, and he and the extremely competent and combative Major Thompson worked out a suitable, if informal, relationship built on mutual respect rooted in powerful first impressions.

A VNMC Battle Group Alpha infantry company boards a U.S. Navy landing craft at the Hue LCU Ramp for a ride to the Citadel. *Courtesy of Ronald Ray*

Chapter 10

MARINES IN THE CITADEL

February 13–20, 1968

The Citadel of Hue was an eerie, confining place for combat Marines whose whole experience in Vietnam had been stomping the bush or occupying rural firebases. The sounds and sights of battles—even during the slack evening hours of February 12, and through the dark, cold night—were somehow more intense, more troubling than these men had experienced in Vietnam. Many of Major Bob Thompson's Marines slept simply because they were exhausted, but many stayed awake that first night in the Citadel and worried about the new prospects for violent death 1/5 faced.

The U.S. Marine battalion's plan of action was simple and direct. According to General Truong's staff, the 1st ARVN Airborne Task Force held a solid line about halfway down the Citadel's northeastern wall, a line that stretched southwest along Mai Thuc Loan Street from the Dong Ba Gate to the northern corner of the Imperial Palace. Though it was short a company and had suffered numerous Tet losses that had not

yet been replaced, 1/5 was still nearly as large as all three ARVN airborne battalions combined. It would march out of the 1st ARVN Division command compound at dawn in column of companies, deploy behind the ARVN line, and mount an immediate attack through the airborne units, directly into the NVA front line.

Leading the battalion tactical march would be Captain Jim Bowe's Alpha/1/5, followed by First Lieutenant Scott Nelson's Charlie/1/5. The battalion command group would follow Nelson's company, and Captain Fern Jennings' Bravo/1/5, in reserve, would bring up the rear of the column.

1/5 moved out of its bivouac at 0800 on February 13. Alpha/1/5 approached the ARVN line from the rear in two columns. About 100 meters along Tinh Tam Street, just as the point was approaching the wall and a tower, a gaggle of ARVN soldiers climbed down from positions atop the wall. These troops laughed and smiled as they passed the Marines.

Marines of 1/5 and a Marine M48 main battle tank prepare to leave the 1st ARVN Division command compound in the northern corner of the Citadel of Hue. February 13. *Official USMC Photo*

The eastern corner of the Citadel of Hue, where 1/5 faced some of the most intense combat of Operation Hue City. *Official USMC Photo*

A 1st Tank Battalion M48, one of five assigned to 1/5, moves past unengaged infantry as it leads a truck toward 1/5's line of departure.
Official USMC Photo by Staff Sergeant Jack Harlan

When the Marine pointman reached the base of the tower, he turned right (southeast) and crossed in front of the entryway. The second man in the column also crossed in front of the entryway. As the third man stepped across, it started to rain grenades from atop the wall.

It was 0815, and the point squad of Alpha/1/5 was still more than 200 meters northwest of what had been billed as the ARVN airborne's front line. Several Marines were wounded. None of the Marines could see the men dropping the grenades, but the rain of explosives was constant for nearly fifteen minutes. The Marines fired blindly the whole time, but the cascade of deadly missiles never abated.

Several more men were injured as they clung to the wall, which loomed a good 20 feet over their heads. Finally it was time to move the wounded back. As several Marines stepped across the tower entryway to collect the unconscious point man, the first NVA soldier anyone had seen atop the wall leaned over the edge and tried to shoot the fallen Marine and his two rescuers. The squad leader emptied an entire M16 magazine into the NVA

soldier and rushed to the rear with the rest of his squad, which took cover in several buildings on the southwestern side of Nguyen Thanh Street.

As the lead squad took cover, another squad tried to enter the gate portal. These Marines were also turned back by the rain of grenades. An M79 grenadier yelled that he could see into the tower and that he was going to shoot at any NVA soldier he could get his sights on. Before the grenadier could fire, Corporal Walter Rosolie streaked across Nguyen Thanh Street alone. Instantly, every Marine set in opposite the tower poured blind suppressive fire into the structure. Rosolie made it to the tower entryway, disarmed an antipersonnel mine he found in the roadway, and lobbed one grenade after another into the tower and up along the top of the wall. He later reported that he had seen NVA soldiers run from the tower, along the wall, but he was unable to enter the structure because other NVA were still in there, firing back at him.

The Marines were simply stunned to have run into such strong opposition so far behind the 1st ARVN Airborne Task Force's front line.

Radio inquiries attempted to get some hard information. It soon became apparent that the ARVN airborne battalions had withdrawn from their advance positions during the night and that elements of the 6th NVA Regiment had advanced into the vacuum.

Caught unaware and off balance, Alpha/1/5 suffered terrible losses. As the Marines groped to find weak spots in the enemy line across their front, the NVA brought more and larger weapons to bear. The Marines responded in kind. An M48 tank was called forward. It pumped five 90mm rounds into the tower with no noticeable effect.

As Captain Bowe searched for a solution and waited for Battalion to decide what to do next, an NVA RPG team sneaked into a position opposite the company command group and let fly one rocket. Bowe, his executive officer, the company gunnery sergeant, and just about everyone around them were injured in the blast.

In all, in the morning meeting engagement, two Alpha/1/5 Marines were killed and thirty-three were wounded. Captain Bowe was replaced by Alpha/1/5's senior platoon commander, an inexperienced second lieutenant.

The NVA had stopped 1/5 cold. Alpha/1/5, which was badly understrength before it reached Hue, was so badly hurt that it had to be withdrawn from the battalion front line to reorganize. Major Thompson ordered Bravo/1/5 forward from its reserve position. Once the company was in place on the left (northeastern) half of Alpha/1/5's line, it was to resume the attack to the southeast. As soon as Bravo jumped off, Charlie/1/5 was to launch a coordinated assault directly through the right half of Alpha/1/5, also toward the former ARVN line, two blocks to the southeast.

While the relief in place and attack preparations were under way—an hours-long job because of enemy fire and unfamiliar conditions—Major

Thompson radioed the 1st Marines command post to request that Delta/1/5 be released from the control of 2/5 and shipped to the Citadel as soon as possible. Regiment said that it would honor the request but that it would be a full day before Delta/1/5 could reach the Citadel.

When Charlie/1/5 jumped off at 1255, it ran straight into NVA automatic-weapons fire bolstered by showers of grenades and many RPGs. The NVA had hurriedly but effectively entrenched themselves within and around many of the buildings facing the Marine company, and they were able to fire their weapons from virtually any angle into all parts of the fragmented platoon formations.

Charlie/1/5 was barely able to inch forward as the novice city fighters trained on the run. Devastating .51-caliber crossfires were the most dangerous hurdles in the crowded streets, where reverberating echoes prevented most Marines from even determining the direction from which the enemy fire was originating. Ricochets were as effective as direct hits, and flying masonry chips were as injurious as bullets.

Heavy casualties were inflicted on Charlie/1/5, just as they had been on every Marine unit facing its first action in the city. But, as in other companies, the survivors learned to cope, learned to shoot first and find targets later, learned to clear rooms with grenades and heavy fire before stepping through doorways, learned to blow open entryways in walls rather than step through doors or climb through windows. The lessons were painful and dearly bought, but they were immutable. One by one, the buildings down the first block facing Charlie/1/5 were reduced and scoured by the increasingly self-assured Marines. Despite heavy and growing losses, Charlie/1/5 continued to press forward.

Even though the NVA had opposed Alpha/1/5 mainly along that company's left flank, along the Citadel wall, Bravo/1/5's renewed attack, which jumped off at the end of the noon hour, met no opposition on that flank until it had advanced nearly two blocks, to a point just 75 meters short of the former ARVN airborne line. At 1330, several M48 tanks sent to support Bravo/1/5 became targets of RPGs, several of which struck home. The tanks pulled back, and Bravo/1/5 halted in place. The damage to the tanks was minor, but temporarily debilitating. One M48 sustained a damaged gunsight, and the other's radio was knocked out.

Two more tanks rolled up behind Bravo/1/5, and the attack resumed through moderate enemy fire. The heaviest resistance came from NVA manning the tower over the Dong Ba Gate—1/5's assigned line of departure—but it was overcome from the street by three LAAWs, four 90mm rounds, and two hundred .50-caliber machine-gun rounds. As soon as the resistance around the Dong Ba tower ceased, Bravo/1/5 patrols scoured the area along the former ARVN airborne front line. No NVA were found, and no casualties were sustained.

In the meantime, Charlie/1/5 broke through the NVA who had been resisting along its front. Or perhaps the NVA, who were flanked by Bravo/1/5, withdrew. Thus, by 1445, 1/5's two assault companies were deployed on a continuous front along Mai Thuc Loan Street, from the Citadel wall to the northern corner of the Imperial Palace.

At 1455, 1st Marines ordered Thompson to stand down for the day and prepare to commence the battalion attack in the morning. To a request

The Dong Ba Gate and tower. At the time this photo was taken, both were in the hands of NVA soldiers. February 14. *Official USMC Photo*

Charlie/1/5 Marines, on 1/5's right flank, infiltrate forward through yards and between buildings. *Official USMC Photo*

intensity of the fight 1/5 faced on its first day in the Citadel. Except for Ernie Cheatham's and Mark Gravel's Hue-blooded companies, no Marines then on active duty had faced anything like the house-to-house street battles 1/5 waded into on February 13. The thin battalion lost many fine combat Marines while learning its way around Hue's mean streets, but it had weathered the worst of the ordeal—the shock and the surprise. Nothing could be worse than the baptism.

*

The situation facing the ARVN, VNMC, and U.S. Marine units inside the Citadel differed considerably from the fighting 2/5 and 1/1 had faced south of the Perfume River. Most of the difference had to do with the compactness of the battlefield. Where 2/5 and 1/1 had had and had used ample room for maneuver, the units inside the Citadel were limited by a number of structures and features that could not be crossed or flanked. The largest and most troublesome of these was the Citadel wall, which was 75 meters thick in some places, and honeycombed throughout by a system of passages and bunkers the Japanese had excavated toward the end of World War II. As Alpha/1/5 learned to its detriment at the outset of its Citadel combat, the wall was a battlefield unto

that he submit a detailed plan by morning, Thompson replied in only five minutes that he would continue the attack as soon as Regiment could get air and artillery—hopefully 155mm and 8-inch fire from Phu Bai—laid on for preparatory fire and on-call support. Thompson also requested that Regiment provide his battalion with tear gas. During the rest of the afternoon, 1/5 improved its positions along Mai Thuc Loan Street and dispatched patrols to the southwest to try to locate friendly units reportedly operating on that flank.

Major Bob Thompson was a tough, tough-minded, thoroughly professional Marine. Although he had spent the six months prior to Tet as a rear-echelon staff officer and had commanded troops in combat for only two weeks, he had trained hard his entire adult life for the job he held in Hue. Nevertheless, nothing—no training and no experience—had prepared him for the complexity and

Firefight along a compound wall. The troops were in as much danger from masonry shards as they were from bullets. *Official USMC Photo*

Priorities. This weary 1/5 rifleman uses a break to clean his weapon rather than try to catch up on his sleep. February 16. *Official USMC Photo*

ARVN 105mm battery at PK 17, to the north. All the American artillery—105mm howitzers, 155mm and 175mm guns, and 8-inch howitzers—was to the south. To hit anything in Hue, all the tubes to the south had to fire pretty much into the faces of the infantry they were supporting. This is important, for everyone involved knew how easy it is to fire artillery "over" the target. In an ideal scenario, artillery fires from behind the troops it is supporting. Second best is where the artillery fires across the front of the troops it is supporting, as was the case where artillery based to the south supported 2/5's attack to the southwest. The close battle quarters in the Citadel and the fact that most of the available supporting artillery was fired toward the friendly front had a chilling effect on the massive use of artillery in the Citadel. Artillery fired from the south was to be used, of course. It *had* to be used, albeit with such caution as to render it less effective than required.

Air support might have made an enormous difference, but there was little or no air support because the weather was lousy. The clouds and fog were so low and the battlefield was so hot that airborne observers could not be used to their full potential because their light, slow spotter planes faced intense small-arms fire below the very low cloud ceilings each new winter day brought forth. Radar-equipped jet fighter-bombers were certainly capable of bombing through the murk, but the limitations of the radar-marking system of the day obviated the pinpoint accuracy required, so the whole concept was passed over. Massively armed American jets and Vietnam Air Force Skyraiders were kept on station over or near Hue, but they had been and would be used only when the pilots could see what they were bombing, rocketing, or strafing—and only if there was adequate room between the target and friendly troops.

*

Despite a less than perfect supporting-arms scenario, 1/5 jumped off again at 0800 on February 14. On the battalion's right, away from the Citadel wall, Charlie/1/5 faced relatively mild

itself, so completely did it dominate the terrain within the Citadel.

Another factor impinging on the options available to Vietnamese and American units attacking from northwest to southeast was the Imperial Palace, the citadel within the Citadel. For reasons of culture and politics, the palace was considered sacrosanct by the Government of Vietnam forces and their allies. NVA and VC firing down from the palace walls could be engaged only by small arms. Moreover, the palace sat roughly in the center of the southeastern half of the Citadel. Its presence channelized the attacking units into two distinct corridors that could not be mutually supported. In effect, in the southeastern half of the Citadel there were two battlefields, isolated from one another and impinged by high walls on either flank.

Early on, another restrictive condition imposed by the orientation of the Citadel battlefield came to light. Virtually all the land-based artillery that could be brought to bear on the NVA-held portions of the Citadel was fired from south of Hue. The exceptions were naval gunfire from the South China Sea, to the east, and an opposition and advanced approximately 100 meters in very short order. On the left, the wall side of the battalion line, Bravo/1/5 got nowhere fast. The NVA who had the previous morning followed the withdrawing ARVN airborne troops back to the northwest had had a full night to retrench around the Dong Ba Gate, and they were immovable. Particularly heavy was the fire from the Dong Ba tower, which Bravo/1/5 had been unable to secure the preceding afternoon. NVA manning the tower completely dominated the two city blocks adjacent to the wall, and the small Marine company could not breast the accurate and intense fire. The Marines and NVA were so closely intermingled at street level that supporting arms—including tanks and 106mm recoilless rifles—could not be effectively employed where it would have mattered most, right along the front line paralleling Mai Thuc Loan Street.

The only reasonable alternative to a toe-to-toe struggle between infantry in the streets was a voluntary withdrawal by 1/5 so massive supporting arms could be employed. Major Thompson and his operations officer drew up a plan, submitted it through Regiment, and began to ease back from the fight along Mai Thuc Loan. The planned artillery and naval gunfire bombardment could not be initiated until all friendly troops were clear of the impact zone, and that did not happen until the middle of the afternoon.

The bombardment began so late that it was decided to continue it through the night. Late in the afternoon, several breaks in the cloud cover allowed several Marine and U.S. Air Force jets to salvo their bombs and rockets against known NVA positions along the northeastern Citadel wall. The air support was effective, but it was limited. While the bombardment was being run, 1/5 consolidated its temporary positions for the night and reorganized and revictualed as much as possible.

*

Late in the afternoon, Captain Myron Harrington's Delta/1/5 was assembled at the Hue LCU Ramp for a quick trip up the river to the

This Charlie/1/5 M60 team has set up its gun to take out NVA snipers in upper stories who are barring the company's advance at ground level. February 16. *Official USMC Photo*

Citadel. Problems arose at the outset when the LCUs arrived chock-a-block with fully loaded resupply trucks and an amazing array of ammunition and gear. Only Captain Harrington squeezed aboard with his company command group and one rifle squad.

Delta/1/5 was temporarily stranded on the wrong side of the river, but as soon as Harrington reached the 1/5 command post, his company was assigned to lead the contemplated dawn assault on the Dong Ba tower.

Late in the day, after a good deal of hectoring from Thompson and arranging by 1st Marines, the balance of Delta/1/5 was lifted to the Citadel aboard three Republic of Vietnam Navy motorized patrol junks. The company main body arrived after 1700, just as Marine fighter-bombers dropped tear gas on the NVA-held portion of the Citadel. An unlucky last-minute shift in the wind carried the gas toward Delta/1/5, and nearly all of

Captain Myron Harrington, of Delta/1/5, earned a Navy Cross for heroic leadership. This photo was taken in 1972, during Harrington's tour as an advisor with the Vietnam Marine Corps. *Courtesy of Colonel Myron Harrington*

1/5's 106mm recoilless rifles could not be used as effectively as those employed south of the Perfume River. There were few vistas long enough for the weapons, and many good targets could not be fired on because of sensitive cultural issues. Nevertheless, when the 106s could be used, they were extremely potent. February 16. *Official USMC Photos*

the approximately one hundred Marines were severely sickened by the fumes. Many Marines hurled themselves into the river to escape the roiling fumes. Once ashore, the company main body drew fire from snipers set outside the Citadel wall.

Delta/1/5 mustered only about a hundred Marines in Hue—a twenty-man platoon had been detached by higher headquarters for convoy-security duty—but it had not been traumatized by the February 13 meeting battles inside the Citadel, as had all three of 1/5's other infantry companies.

*

On the northwestern side of the Citadel, where ARVN units were locked in battle with another extremely stubborn NVA force, elements of the 3d ARVN Regiment, two battle-weakened troops of the 7th ARVN Armored Cavalry Battalion, the 1st ARVN Division's Hoc Bao Company, and even the 1st ARVN Ordnance

Company had been fought to a virtual standstill more than a week before the arrival of VNMC Battle Group Alpha. The ARVN units had not been able to advance from the vicinity of Tay Loc Airfield, the ordnance company's armory, and the Chanh Tay Gate, but neither had the NVA units squabbling over the same area been able to advance. Each side had hurt the other, but neither had been able to gain the upper hand in what became a classic static battle of attrition. The two newly arrived VNMC battalions were to put things right and press the NVA back, particularly in the center, where the ordnance company was holding secure a store of 1,400 M16 rifles and hundreds of other weapons.

Battle Group Alpha had expected to launch a two-battalion attack to the southeast, between the southwestern Citadel wall and the Imperial Palace, as soon as it arrived on February 12, but

the situation in the 3d ARVN Regiment zone was so chaotic, and friendly holdings were so checkered, that it took the Vietnamese marines and their ARVN compatriots two full days to establish a line of departure. In fact, the NVA attacked the relatively weak 1st Battalion, 3d ARVN Regiment, in such strength near the Chanh Tay Gate that the ARVN unit was surrounded and cut off. The Hoc Bao Company and an armored cavalry troop had to be diverted to attack through the enemy cordon, a process that would ultimately require two days of battle.

The sum of all the line-straightening and the rescue operation was that Battle Group Alpha did not reach a position from which it could launch its attack to the southeast until the evening of February 14. Even then, there were enemy troops to the rear—and no end of enemy troops to the front. Indeed, by then, elements of several NVA infantry battalions newly arrived from Khe Sanh as well as ample fresh supplies were being infiltrated into the Citadel via the unsecured Huu Gate. As many reinforcements as General Truong could bring in, the NVA could see and raise.

*

While a predawn final artillery preparation raged against objectives all along 1/5's former front, Charlie/1/5 and Bravo/1/5 closed up to the right and Delta/1/5 slid in between Bravo/1/5's left flank and the Citadel's northeastern wall. As soon as the preparatory fires were lifted at 0800, all three U.S. Marine companies jumped off into the ceded block northwest of Mai Thuc Loan Street. As expected, Charlie/1/5 and Bravo/1/5 quickly and efficiently advanced into the twisted rubble and regained all of the ground they had given up the previous afternoon. As hoped, the resistance the NVA defenders put up on 1/5's center and right was noticeably weaker than 1/5 had yet faced in the Citadel. For all that, however, Delta/1/5 ran into a hornet's nest as it attempted to close on the Dong Ba tower.

Delta/1/5's late arrival on February 14 and the ongoing artillery preparation had prevented

Captain Harrington and his troop leaders from reconnoitering the objective, even at long range. So as Delta/1/5 jumped off into the attack on February 15, it did so without any real knowledge of the ground or the locations of any enemy positions. One early result was that the young lieutenant commanding Delta/1/5's 2d Platoon advanced to a second-story balcony facing the Dong Ba tower, the better to control the fight. In a flash, the lieutenant, his platoon sergeant, his radio operator, and at least one of his platoon's squad leaders were injured by an RPG. The platoon remained in the fight, but Harrington was unable to communicate instantaneously with the platoon guide, now in command of the unit, until a replacement radio could be scrounged.

As Harrington and others in Delta/1/5 quickly learned, verbal communication of any sort was severely hampered by the volume of gunfire that echoed across the restricted masonry battlefield. If Delta/1/5 had arrived in the Citadel confident of its baptism south of the Perfume, it was

A Delta/1/5 M60 gunner perched on an ornate roof goes head-to-head with NVA troops dug in across the way.
Official USMC Photo by Corporal D. Fisher

quickly disabused of the notion. The intense close-quarters battle for the Citadel was nothing at all like the company's two-day south-side walk in the sun while attached to 2/5.

Bravo/1/5 and Charlie/1/5 fought their way back to Mai Thuc Loan Street pretty much because the NVA conceded the ground. Delta/1/5 was fought to a standstill well short of Mai Thuc Loan and the Dong Ba tower because the NVA were unwilling to give up the "high ground" the tower and the wall represented.

The big break came at about 1400, when Captain Harrington resorted to the obvious. One infantry squad climbed onto the wall about 150 meters northwest of the Dong Ba tower and opened a methodical sweep along the high ground. This was not a matter of running along a narrow rampart; the wall was up to 75 meters thick along the way, and every bit as heavily built up as the streets below.

As the squad on the wall registered some modest gains against stiffening opposition, Delta/1/5 Marines on the more lightly engaged company right sent over scarce hand grenades in response to shouted appeals for more of what was proving to be the most expedient weapon on the narrow high-ground battlefield.

Atop the wall and on the street, every available 3.5-inch rocket launcher was arrayed directly against the tower and the Japanese-built, NVA-held bunkers and pillboxes inside the wall adjacent to the Dong Ba Gate. Delta/1/5's 60mm mortars also were brought to bear exclusively on the gate and tower strongpoint, and they were fired incessantly down to danger-close ranges.

The M48 gun tanks were also extremely effective. By a miracle of coincidence, the extremely snug streets inside the Citadel—they had no sidewalks—could just accommodate the width of an M48 tank with literally a few inches to spare. While the other tanks and a pair of Ontos worked farther from the wall, the tank platoon commander gingerly guided his command M48 behind Delta/1/5 and found a covered spot about 25 meters from the gate, just behind the building Captain Harrington was using for his company command and observation post. At frequent intervals, the tank ran right into Mai Thuc Loan and, while the platoon commander fired his cupola-mounted .50-caliber machine gun to suppress NVA RPG teams, the gunner brought the 90mm main gun around to a new target and fired right at the wall and the tower. Often as not, the gunner took his directions via radio from Captain Harrington, who was never more than a few meters away. At first Harrington thought of using the field telephone that was affixed to one of the tank's rear fenders (a standard procedure), but the tank was raked by NVA bullets as soon as it appeared in the intersection the first time—and every time thereafter—so Harrington opted for the less reliable radio.

The tanks, rockets, and mortars were deadly accurate whenever they were employed, but the NVA were bitterly determined to hold their strongpoint. The best fighting positions were remanned as quickly as they were rearranged.

A Marine sharpshooter equipped with a 7.62mm M14 rifle takes careful aim at his prey. February 18. *Official USMC Photo*

As Delta/1/5 struggled forward on and along the wall, Charlie/1/5's easy morning advance was stalled in the early afternoon by NVA machine guns set in atop and within the northern corner of the Imperial Palace. Had the NVA machine guns been set in anywhere else in Hue, they would have been blasted to dust by Marine artillery or naval gunfire, or even by 1/5's mortars. But the Imperial Palace was inviolate to American explosive munitions. The Charlie/1/5 Marines were permitted to return the fire with their M16s and M60s, but the only explosives that could be placed on the Imperial Palace had to be fired by ARVN or VNMC units. The only ARVN 105mm battery north of Hue was busy with other missions, and the VNMC 81mm mortars and six 105mm howitzers were in hot action against Battle Group Alpha's own objectives, so nothing could be done to help Charlie/1/5. Thus Charlie/1/5's February 15 advance bogged down. When that happened, Major Thompson ordered the company to halt in place and refuse its right flank about a hundred meters to prevent the NVA from infiltrating the 1/5 zone from that quarter. To help, Thompson sent Delta/1/5's 3d Platoon, which had just arrived in Hue from a stint of convoy-escort duty to the south.

There were no ARVN or VNMC units for several hundred meters to Charlie/1/5's right, but there were plenty of NVA out there. The result was that it took most of the rest of the day for Charlie/1/5 to clear a buffer zone and emplace the Delta/1/5 platoon in a number of buildings back along the flank.

In the battalion center, Bravo/1/5 reached Mai Thuc Loan early but had to stop because Delta/1/5 could not come abreast on the left and Charlie/1/5 became bogged down as it tried to advance toward the Imperial Palace farther on the right. Thus, by the early afternoon of February 15, 1/5's three front-line companies were on or behind the line of departure that was supposed to have been left behind on February 13.

The Delta/1/5 squad on the wall—bolstered many times over by Marines replacing wounded

This Marine rifleman is taking cover, and a break, behind a garden wall. February 18. *Official USMC Photo*

Marines—reached the base of the Dong Ba tower at about 1600. By then, the tower was barely more than a higher pile of rubble, and it was still infested with NVA soldiers clearly intent upon defending it unto death.

Before the attack could bog down from sheer loss of momentum, Captain Harrington engineered a quick final assault with troops readily at hand. Fortunately, Delta/1/5 was reinforced at the last minute from the battalion right by a thin squad of the company's own newly arrived 3d Platoon.

Covered by a barrage of twenty 60mm mortar rounds placed squarely atop the objective, the main body of the 1st Platoon jumped off at 1630 from positions just south of the tower. In a matter of minutes, the Marines overran the Dong Ba Gate's archway and bridge at street level.

In all on February 15, 1/5 lost six Marines killed and thirty-three wounded and evacuated. The Marines pulled twenty-four NVA and VC corpses from the rubble.

*

On the southwestern side of the battlefield, the 1st and 5th VNMC battalions secured the 1st

ARVN Ordnance Company armory and swung about to begin a two-column attack to the southeast, paralleling 1/5's move. The VNMC battalions faced pitiless resistance throughout the day in their parallel zones, and each sustained heavy losses. But by day's end, they held a line two blocks northwest of the Imperial Palace. This line was separated from the 1/5 line by a no-man's-land several hundred meters wide.

In all on February 15, Battle Group Alpha recovered thirty-nine dead NVA soldiers and assorted infantry weapons and munitions. It is possible that the Vietnamese Marines also killed a high-ranking NVA officer, possibly the commander of the 6th NVA Regiment.

As the Vietnamese marines advanced deeper into what had been enemy territory from the outset of the Tet Offensive in Hue, they came upon increasing evidence that Communist hit squads were hard at work. Fresh civilian corpses bearing execution-type gunshot wounds began turning up almost from the outset of the VNMC attack. Other civilian corpses were disinterred from graves in which they apparently had been buried alive.

*

The 4th VNMC Battalion, which had weathered bitter fighting in Saigon for most of the previous two weeks, had arrived in Phu Bai by air late on February 14. It mustered seven hundred effectives (of whom two hundred had been assigned to the unit only two days earlier), but it arrived in Phu Bai with only two jeeps. The demands upon U.S. Marine Corps transportation assets in the region were overwhelming, so it took most of February 15 to muster enough trucks for the entire VNMC battalion. By then it was too late to depart Phu Bai, but it was a virtual certainty that the fresh, extremely hard-fighting 4th VNMC Battalion would reach the Citadel early on February 16.

It was hoped by South Vietnamese and American commanders alike that the insertion of a third strong VNMC battalion on the Battle Group Alpha front would allow the Vietnamese and U.S. Marines to link up in the center of the Citadel battlefield and thus allow major elements of the reinforced 3d ARVN Regiment to stand down and reorganize.

*

At about 0430, February 16, the NVA bombarded Delta/1/5's Dong Ba tower position with 82mm and 60mm mortars. Then a volley of grenades and RPGs forced the five Delta/1/5 Marines in the tower itself to withdraw. In no time, the NVA opened fire from the tower, down upon the main body of Delta/1/5. Captain Myron Harrington organized an instant counter-counterattack, using whatever troops he could lead into the fray on instantaneous notice. As Harrington fired his .45-caliber pistol at point-blank range, Marines who regained a position at the base of the tower lobbed hand grenades at the NVA who were firing at them from above. LAAWs, M79 grenades, and intense small-arms fire eventually turned the tide. The tower was secured again, but sporadic fighting continued around the Dong Ba Gate until dawn. When the NVA finally withdrew, they left two of their comrades dead in the tower. Delta/1/5 lost one Marine killed and four Marines wounded in the fray.

*

February 16 dawned relatively fair and clear over Hue. For the first time since the struggle for Hue began, air support could be routinely scheduled into the morning's preparatory pounding, which also included naval gunfire from the east and heavy artillery from the south. The NVA responded with what they had. At 0655, Bravo/1/5 and Delta/1/5 were engaged by NVA small-arms fire and several RPGs. The Marines responded in kind and also fired sixty-eight 81mm mortar rounds into the buildings from which the NVA were firing. Enemy casualties could not be estimated, but two Marines were killed and seven were wounded.

1/5 jumped off at dawn. Delta/1/5, on the left, was the first company to cross Mai Thuc Loan Street, but it immediately met stiff resist-

In the midst of 1/5's intense house-to-house battle, a Marine emerges from a wrecked home with a wounded and emaciated Vietnamese girl in his arms. *Texas Tech Virtual Vietnam Archive/Douglas Pike Photo Collection*

ance along the wall, in an area that, for purposes of safety, could not be included in the morning's bombardment coverage.

Bravo/1/5, in the battalion center, also ran into extremely stiff opposition from an area that had not been covered by the morning bombardment. The NVA remained well entrenched in a rat's nest of fighting holes, pillboxes, and bunkers set into the ruins of many masonry buildings. There was no way to conduct an orderly or even very methodical advance into the twisted rubble.

On the far right, Charlie/1/5 once again met light resistance. There is no doubt that the company could have advanced deep into enemy territory, but the decision was made to keep its progress down to the pace of the two companies to its left, because Charlie/1/5 was still responsible for screening 1/5's open right flank. As the tempo

of the fighting increased in the adjacent Bravo/1/5 zone, more Charlie/1/5 troops were shifted toward the battalion's center to support the struggling center company with small-arms fire.

In all on February 16, 1/5 lost twelve Marines killed, forty-five wounded and evacuated, and fifteen wounded and returned to duty. The battalion turned in a claim for twenty-six NVA killed and fourteen assorted weapons and a former Marine field radio captured.

*

The 4th VNMC Battalion arrived at the Hue LCU Ramp by truck from Phu Bai late in the morning on February 16. The trip across the river was painless. The battalion mustered at the quay and marched straight into the 1st ARVN Division command compound. No sooner done than the battalion was sent into the attack to relieve pressure on the 1st Battalion, 3d ARVN Regiment, which remained pinned to positions around the Chanh Tay Gate.

The 4th VNMC Battalion faced many NVA who sniped from within multistory buildings with all manner of small arms, RPGs, and many .51-caliber heavy machine guns. Unlike their U.S. Marine counterparts, the Vietnamese marines had few weapons—only a few captured RPGs—that could punch through masonry walls, so the only way to advance was up the streets, and that, in the face of expertly sited .51-caliber fire, took more guts than can be explained.

At day's end, the 4th VNMC Battalion still had not reached the Citadel's western corner. Overnight, however, the NVA force that had held the Chanh Tay Gate melted away. No doubt, the pressure represented by a fresh seven-hundred-man VNMC battalion was enough to convince the Communist troops to leave the shattered 1st Battalion, 3d ARVN Regiment, in peace.

*

At 2150, the 1/5 command group received mixed news from enemy sources. A message from 1st Marines stated: "Message intercepted from enemy radio message [from] the commander of the enemy force inside Hue to his superior states that original commander of the force inside Hue had been killed and that many others had either been killed or wounded. He recommended to withdraw. Senior officer ordered new commander of the force in Hue to remain in position and fight."

It was heartening for many Marines to learn that the enemy commander had been killed, but the fact that the new commander on the scene had been rebuffed in his efforts to have his unit withdrawn was not good news at all. It smacked of a fanatical desire by the Communist regional commander, for there was no doubt that the Communist forces would be driven from Hue. The only things lacking in that regard were a timetable and a count of how many deaths it would take. All this so the NLF flag could fly over the Citadel wall for a few days longer.

*

For 1/5, the February 17 action began at 0430, when Delta/1/5 was struck by a mortar barrage originating from an NVA-occupied but uncontested sector east of the Citadel, across the

Perfume River. As the mortar barrage lifted, NVA dug in along the company's immediate front opened fire with RPGs and small arms. The Marines responded with M16s, M60s, M79s, and LAAWs, and finally called an 8-inch howitzer mission for good measure. As the 8-inch shells landed, the NVA broke contact. The result of the two-step wake-up call was one Marine killed, four Marines wounded and evacuated, and two NVA soldiers known dead.

1/5 waded into the NVA defensive zone beginning at 0700. The advance was slow but steady against mutually supporting pockets—rather than a continuous line—of resistance. As they had during 2/5's final sweep between the Perfume River and the Phu Cam Canal, the NVA resorted to delaying tactics centered on the unyielding defense of strongly fortified, mutually supporting strongpoints. Initially this arrangement gave the ever-smaller Marine companies, platoons, and squads more latitude for maneuvering than had previously been the case, and each strongpoint was reduced in turn, albeit at great

The thin remainder of Bravo/1/5's 1st Platoon takes a break in a walled compound. February 19. *Official USMC Photo*

Delta/1/5 Marines kick down a brick wall so they can proceed in the attack from one building compound to the next. At left is an Associated Press photographer. February 19. *Official USMC Photo*

arrayed along Han Thuyen Street, exactly halfway down the Imperial Palace's northeastern wall and three blocks from the Thuong Tu Gate.

In response to 1/5's repeated and ever-stronger pleas for reinforcements, sixty-two replacements were helilifted into the Citadel between 1617 and 1640, February 17. The boost was needed, but sixty-two replacements hardly made a dent in the battalion's manpower needs. In fact, the new men did not even make good that one day's losses. The cumulative results of the February 17 fighting alone amounted to twelve Marines killed and fifty-five wounded and evacuated. Against this, 1/5 counted twenty-eight NVA confirmed killed.

*

Also on February 17, the 4th VNMC Battalion reached the Citadel's western corner against sporadic rear-guard resistance. When the area within the corner and around the Chanh Tay Gate had been thoroughly scoured, the 4th VNMC Battalion relieved the cut-up ARVN battalions that had been fighting there for two weeks. The VNMC battalion received orders to continue mopping up around the Chanh Tay Gate on February 18. Then, if everything went well, it would join Battle Group Alpha on February 19 for the final assault toward the southern corner of the Citadel.

*

1/5 could not continue its attack on February 18. In addition to its diminished capacity for just enduring the day's extremely cold and wet weather conditions, the U.S. Marine battalion had run critically low of ammunition of all types. Moreover, its infantry companies each mustered far fewer than a hundred Marines apiece. The battalion had been in contact with enemy forces for most of the past forty-five days, and its internal organization needed some extensive revamping. So critical was the shortage of all types of supplies that the troops had not been fed adequately—in some cases, not at all—on February 17, and they experienced another day of the same on February 18. Compounding all

expense in time and dwindling manpower. On the other hand, as 1/5 advanced, NVA automatic weapons emplaced atop the Imperial Palace's northeastern wall were able to lay upon the front, rear, and flanks of the American platoons and squads. The Marines were allowed to return this fire with their M60s and M16s, but not with any of their explosive ordnance, and that definitely had a chilling effect on the advance that offset most other advantages. Some ARVN and VNMC artillery was called in against the Imperial Palace wall, but it was limited in strength and duration and thus of limited value. By the middle of the afternoon, Charlie/1/5 was obliged to tie up one of its small platoons to cordon off the palace wall while the remainder of the battalion sideslipped a block away and bypassed the most active strongpoints along its top. The decision to use even eighteen or twenty Marines to man static positions nearly overtaxed 1/5's extremely limited and constantly dwindling manpower resources. Nevertheless, by the time 1/5 stopped for the day, at 1630, its three front-line companies were

Alpha/1/5 Marines place captured AK-47s and magazines on a display table. Almost every fallen Communist position yielded dead Communist fighters and their weapons. February 19. *Official USMC Photo by Corporal John Pennington*

those problems, the battalion's supporting arms had run out of their comfort zone. With 1/5's front line only a few blocks from the Citadel's southeastern wall, there was no longer any effective means for adjusting large-caliber fire missions without seriously endangering the troops calling for the support.

General Truong somewhat alleviated the constraints of 1/5's virtually overwhelming manpower shortages on February 18 by dispatching the battle-weakened but otherwise formidable Hoc Bao and 1st ARVN Division Reconnaissance companies to the U.S. Marine battalion's right flank, along the Imperial Palace wall. As soon as the Hoc Bao Company reached the 1/5 command post, the company commander asked Major Thompson to blow a hole in the Palace's northeastern gate so his tiger-suited soldiers could assault the citadel within the Citadel. Thompson admired the ARVN captain's courage, but he refused the request. There was no way even the elite Hoc Bao Company could survive such an attack, much less prevail. When the captain insisted that he was under direct orders from General Truong to carry out the assault, Thompson radioed the 1st ARVN Division commander and begged him to rescind

This 1/5 Marine looks too tired and worn down to even get on the floor to sleep. *Official USMC Photo*

the order. Truong readily agreed to Thompson's request.

Though 1/5 remained rooted to its line along the northwestern side of Han Thuyen Street on February 18, the battalion nevertheless accounted for a considerable number of enemy soldiers, albeit at a high cost.

*

Both the 1st and the 5th VNMC battalions were much stronger than 1/5, but they were both less well equipped and less physically acclimated to February 18's extremely bitter weather conditions. Despite the best efforts of their officers and enlisted leaders to get them going, the thoroughly weather-beaten junior Vietnamese marines were able to muster only feeble efforts to advance.

Late in the afternoon, the equally wet, miserable, and unacclimated 4th VNMC Battalion slid into position on Battle Group Alpha's right flank, along Thuy Quan Canal, and the 1st VNMC Battalion went into reserve. If the weather—or something—improved by the next morning, Battle Group Alpha would kick off what was being billed as the final assault to clear the southwest quadrant of the Citadel. Overall, more than 1,200 VNMC infantrymen were arrayed to attack an area just as large as the area that was under attack by 1/5, a force no larger than 400 U.S. Marine infantry effectives, and the Hoc Bao and 1st ARVN Division Reconnaissance companies, which, combined, mustered fewer than 200 effectives.

*

February 19 was more of the same. Following a day of relative rest, 1/5's three hungry, exhausted front-line companies jumped off again, but feebly. The NVA had all the advantages of position and time, and there might have been more of them holding their array of strongpoints than there were Marines and ARVN soldiers on that side of the Citadel to seize the strongpoints.

By February 19, the NVA were holding such a compact area that 1/5's attack was less the reduction of a built-up city area than an assault

on a fortified position, a different animal entirely. Major Thompson later likened the fighting during this period as being closer in nature to Tarawa than to Seoul. The *whole* objective was really just one big strongpoint, complete with interlocking bands of fire and no end of mutually supporting fighting positions. Moreover, the defenders literally had their backs to a wall, so their at times fanatical resistance was the only alternative to annihilation. Even on the brink of defeat, the NVA facing 1/5 were first-rate veterans.

The U.S. Marine battalion lacked any room for maneuver. The only way to defeat the defenders was by means of an endless series of expensive frontal assaults. Forced to employ just this one graceless tactic, crowded into a very small zone of action, weak in numbers and diluted by (not enough) inexperienced replacements, inadequately resupplied, and unable to take advantage of its usual supporting-arms superiority, 1/5 was simply unable to get any steam up. Despite the availabil-

ity of a huge array of heavy-caliber, long-range artillery and several relatively mobile warships, the only useful or safe-to-use supporting arms that were really available to 1/5 were its own 81mm mortars and 106mm recoilless rifles, the infantry companies' own 60mm mortars and 3.5-inch rocket launchers, a pair of 4.2-inch mortars set in at MACV, a platoon of five M48 gun tanks, and two Ontos. Even if there had been adequate supplies of munitions for them—there never was—most of these weapons either did not pack enough punch or have enough range to really bombard the NVA strongpoints to submission. And there were not enough streetwise Marine infantrymen led by experienced officers and non-commissioned officers left to do the job wholly by means of direct assault.

Major Thompson considered the tanks and Ontos his most important assets. The tanks were able to take a pretty fair licking, but the Ontos were unbelievably vulnerable. Nevertheless, their

A Charlie/1/5 M60 team "works out." February 19. *Official USMC Photo by Corporal John Pennington*

106mm recoilless rifles, fired in any combination from one to six, were easily the most effective weapons on the battlefield, superb for tackling masonry houses the NVA were turning into bunkers. The trick was to get an Ontos into firing position without getting it blown away. The solution was produced by the tank platoon commander, who teamed one or two tanks with each Ontos. Then, at Thompson's express order, whenever infantrymen came up against a target they thought was worth risking an Ontos to blow down, the infantry commander had to request an Ontos via the battalion command post. The Ontos and tank commanders then had to conduct a personal reconnaissance of the target on foot with the infantry commander. If the target could be fired on without undue risk, the Ontos commander laid out the plan. Generally, the infantrymen fired all the suppression they could, the tank nosed up and fired its main gun and machine guns, and while the NVA had their heads down, the tank withdrew and the Ontos zipped up, fired all its 106s, and reversed through the backblast. Every M48 tank attached to 1/5 took ten or twelve hits apiece, and many tank crewmen were wounded or killed. None of the Ontos supporting 1/5 were ever hit, and none of the Ontos crewmen were injured by enemy fire.

Perhaps the worst liability facing 1/5 was the prohibition against firing effectively at NVA positions within and atop the Imperial Palace walls. The Hoc Bao and 1st ARVN Division Reconnaissance companies were to have taken care of opposition on that flank, but their presence never really came to anything because the elite ARVN companies did not have access to effective supporting-arms assets. As long as NVA machine guns and snipers could fire into 1/5's rear and flanks with virtual impunity, 1/5 could not effectively advance. This is not to say that the U.S. Marines honored the letter of the law, as tanks and Ontos did fire at the palace wall when there were clear targets; it just meant that effective means for quelling the wall positions—

reducing them and their occupants to dust— could not be employed.

Adding to the general mayhem was the need to consider the safety of many hundreds of civilians who were crowding in behind the battalion, waiting to return to what was left of their homes. Several sniping incidents behind 1/5 convinced Major Thompson that there were NVA and VC infiltrators among the refugees, but there was nothing he could do. There were too many people for his Marines to interrogate or even cordon off from access to the battlefield. In the end, Thompson assigned the 2d Battalion, 3d ARVN Regiment, to handle the refugees. The U.S. Marines did their best to ignore the civilians and their plight, but they were there and they were a factor.

The net effect of all the mounting problems was that 1/5 made little progress on either February 19 or February 20. The U.S. Marines claimed the lives of many NVA soldiers, but they sustained casualties in kind. They overran NVA strongpoints, but they could not find the key to breaking into and overcoming the NVA defensive sector. In two days of heavy fighting—and after sustaining more heavy losses—1/5 stood only one block farther into the NVA defensive zone. Far from battling it out on equal terms with a demoralized, defeated 6th NVA Regiment rearguard, 1/5 found itself collecting documents from the bodies of members of the 5th NVA Regiment, the 324B NVA Division's 90th NVA Regiment, and the 325C NVA Division's 29th NVA Regiment. Far from defeating the shattered and fragmented 6th NVA Regiment in place, the U.S. Marines and their ARVN and VNMC allies suddenly found themselves facing a seemingly inexhaustible supply of fresh combat-experienced NVA soldiers.

In a week's fighting, by dusk on February 20, 1/5 had sustained a total of 47 Marines and corpsmen killed, 240 Marines and corpsmen wounded and evacuated, and 60 Marines and corpsmen wounded and returned to duty. Nobody knew how many Marines and corpsmen had simply kept their injuries hidden to avoid being evacuated from their units.

By the end of the day, February 20, Alpha/1/5 was down to about seventy effectives, Bravo/1/5 was down to about eighty effectives, and Charlie/1/5 and Delta/1/5 were not much better off. Only two platoons in the entire battalion were commanded by officers, and all three of Bravo/1/5's platoons were led by corporals. The troops had not been adequately fed in four days, and there was never enough of the right kinds of munitions.

*

1/5 was slipping. Bob Thompson saw it happening, but there was nothing he could do beyond yelling at higher headquarters to get the types of help he needed—food, ammunition, replacements, permission to level the Imperial Palace walls, and some way to seal the city against the further infiltration of NVA reinforcements. Higher headquarters yelled back. At one point Thompson became so fed up with prodding radio messages from seniors who had never deigned to visit in person that he asked one of them to find his replacement. The senior officer backed off.

The only bright news on Thompson's horizon was that the 5th Marines commander was trying to get a company of 3/5 moved up from southern I Corps to attach to 1/5. In fact, late on February 20, Lima/3/5 was alerted for the move, which was to commence in stages the next day.

*

At 0430, February 19, the NVA struck the 5th VNMC Battalion sector with three hundred 82mm mortar rounds and many RPGs, and then they launched a large, well-coordinated infantry assault. Only the effective use of the VNMC 105mm battery, which fired more than two thousand rounds—nearly its entire ready supply—prevented the NVA reserve from attacking through breaches ripped into the VNMC line by the NVA assault force. The NVA attack was beaten back with enormous losses—estimated as high as 150

NVA killed—and the 5th VNMC Battalion's line was fully restored.

The 4th and 5th VNMC battalions resumed the Battle Group Alpha attack on schedule but made no progress. The reinforced NVA units inside the Citadel had adequate reason to stall 1/5, but they were frankly out to humiliate the Government of Vietnam troops fighting in the Citadel. Political goals aside, however, the entire NVA reinforcement and resupply effort—and any possible organized withdrawal—required the availability of the Huu Gate through the Citadel wall, so the NVA naturally put most of their effort into stopping the VNMC advance.

For all the resistance the VNMC battalions encountered, all was not well with the NVA forces inside the Citadel. Beginning late in the day on February 19, and on into February 20, VNMC officers monitoring NVA radio frequencies reported that high-ranking NVA and VC military and political officers were disappearing from their command post inside the Imperial Palace. There were even indications that several NVA combat units had been ordered to clear out of the Citadel before the Huu Gate was sealed.

The South Vietnamese forces pretty much halted in place on February 20 so arrangements could be made to bring psychological warfare experts and their equipment to the forward battle lines. The development was surprising and maddening to most Americans on the scene, but it was entirely consistent with Vietnamese values. Sensing that they were standing on the brink of a major political victory, the Government of Vietnam forces could not only afford to be magnanimous to their enemies, they also had much to gain by offering easy surrender terms. If the remaining NVA and VC gave up without a fight, more physical damage—particularly to the Imperial Palace—would be obviated, and lives would be saved. The impact of the political victory would be boosted many times over by the government's ability to show off former Communists and Communist sympathizers who had rallied to the forces of freedom.

Chapter 11

THE
FLAGPOLE

February 21–24, 1968

Beginning at 2300 hours, February 20, Alpha/1/5's reinforced but nonetheless minuscule 2d Platoon infiltrated the NVA front line to the area around the Thuong Tu Gate. By 0330 the platoon was safely ensconced in several multistory buildings astride the gate.

At 0800 members of the patrol manning observation posts spotted two NVA units gathering in the open on either side of the Marine-held enclave. The 81mm forward observer who had accompanied the patrol—he was the main reason for its being there—ordered a tear-gas mission by the section of 4.2-inch mortars set in at MACV. Both groups of NVA dispersed. Then a scout-sniper team that was also on the mission went to work, using the confusion triggered by the tear gas to work their trade without drawing attention. The snipers killed four NVA at that time, and many others in due course. The patrol's position was never compromised.

When news of the foray got around—Major Bob Thompson insisted that the other companies tune in to Alpha/1/5's company net—the entire battalion became suffused with enthusiasm. Here was an object lesson that Marines could be as skilled in infiltration tactics as the NVA they faced.

*

Throughout the day, the NVA facing the main body of 1/5 resisted at long range with machine guns and rifles. Marines attacking toward the southeastern wall saw few NVA, but they felt the sting of the enemy's presence. Captain Myron Harrington's dwindling Delta/1/5 tried time and again to advance along the top of the northeastern wall to the Citadel's eastern corner but made no net gains. Bravo/1/5 and the main body of Delta/1/5 jumped off into a renewed assault at 1111 hours, but they were held to minimal gains. Toward the end of the day, Charlie/1/5 was driven to ground by intense NVA fire. The entire NVA defensive sector was honeycombed with stoutly built fighting positions.

Snipers on both sides seemed more numerous and became more effective as the battlefield inside the Citadel became smaller. This 5th Marines sniper has set up a nest on the top floor of a building in the Delta/1/5 zone. *Official USMC Photo by Corporal John Pennington*

Lima/3/5 Marines, new to urban combat, have been driven to ground by Communist fire. *Official USMC Photo by Corporal John Pennington*

U.S. Army "Bird Dog" spotter planes carrying Marine infantry officers serving as aerial observers were able to run few air strikes until the afternoon of February 22. They typically flew low and slow, the better to spot targets and assess damage. One of the Bird Dog pilots was killed at the controls on February 22, and the Marine aerial observer was seriously burned. *Official USMC Photo by Lance Corporal D. M. Messenger*

The cumulative losses sustained by 1/5 on February 21 were three Marines killed, fourteen wounded and evacuated, and five wounded and returned to duty. Against these totals, sixteen NVA or VC were confirmed killed and one NVA soldier surrendered. At day's end, for all the stiff resistance, elements of 1/5 stood within a block of the Citadel's southeastern wall.

Through the day and into a second night the Alpha/1/5 patrol remained unmolested in the buildings it had occupied around the Thuong Tu Gate.

*

At 0930, February 21, Captain John Niotis's Lima/3/5 was attached to the 1st Marines, and at 1435 the company was formally attached to 1/5 for use in the Citadel. Immediately, the relatively fresh unit was collected in Doc Lao Park for a helilift into the 1st ARVN Division command compound. The first lift was fired on by NVA machine guns, and so was a subsequent lift, after which the effort was called off, leaving the last forty-five members of Lima/3/5 stranded at MACV for the night.

*

Battle Group Alpha remained in position behind the Thuy Quan Canal, only halfway along the Citadel's southwest wall. The VNMC

This Lima/3/5 rifleman has found a long vista inside the Citadel and is searching for a target. *Official USMC Photo by Corporal John Pennington*

battalions simply could not make headway. Impeded by the canal, which ran the full length of their front, attacks by both VNMC front-line battalions were partly channelized on two bridges, and the VNMC position was completely dominated by NVA machine guns on the Citadel wall. When the Vietnamese Marines tried tear gas on the defenders in front of them, the NVA used issue cloth or field-expedient gas masks that seemed to offset the effects of the gas. When the VNMC ground assault kicked off in the wake of the gas attack, the NVA were able to defeat it. Later, 122mm rockets no doubt

A napalm canister detonates on a suspected NVA position between the Citadel wall and the Perfume River. *Official USMC Photo by Lance Corporal D. M. Messenger*

fired from the high hills to the west fell into the Battle Group Alpha zone, where they inflicted additional casualties.

It was entirely logical that the NVA put their major effort against Battle Group Alpha, because it was the VNMC battalions that stood poised to capture the Huu Gate, the 6th NVA Regiment's last unobstructed portal through the Citadel wall. There were still many soldiers and VC sympathizers to evacuate from the Citadel, and the members of the proposed Communist municipal and provincial governments were apparently still there on February 21. Moreover, the terrain facing Battle Group Alpha lent itself to the type of defensive effort at which the NVA were most skilled. The ground facing the 4th VNMC Battalion, for example, was parkland dotted with homes and temples—ideal terrain for the defender, particularly in light of the high Citadel wall that prevented the 4th VNMC Battalion from maneuvering around the kilometer-deep NVA-defended area.

On the plus side, the VNMC battalions had almost more artillery support than they could use. Thompson's 1/5 could not call much more than mortars to hit the restricted zone to its front, but the Vietnamese marines had access to their own 105mm howitzer battery, all manner of U.S. heavy artillery, and even U.S. naval gunfire support. So though the VNMC battalions could not advance, they could take part in killing or maiming many NVA and in restricting the flow of Communist refugees through the Huu Gate. Moreover, by day's end it was obvious that four U.S. Army battalions arrayed northwest of Hue would be free to press in upon the Communist evacuation and reinforcement routes from outside the Citadel.

For all that, Battle Group Alpha was hurt and out of steam. The key to its breaking

through the Communist line was air support, but the weather continued to obviate that option.

*

In addition to the pressure the U.S. Army battalions were bound to provide from the outside, the generally favorable situation throughout I Corps had allowed the ARVN corps commander to agree to send two hitherto embattled ARVN Ranger battalions—part of the I Corps strategic reserve—to Hue. Both battalions were dispatched via PK 17 that night, and the 1st ARVN Division assigned them to clearing VC cadres out of the built-up areas on the eastern bank of the Perfume River.

Marines unloading supplies at the Hue LCU Ramp must wear gas masks to neutralize tear gas that is drifting across the Perfume River from the embattled Citadel. *Official USMC Photo by Gunnery Sergeant R. W. Thompson*

Combat engineers attached to 1/5 fight their way forward through a zone covered by NVA snipers. *Official USMC Photo*

Much of the battle inside the Citadel was fought on little or no sleep. Here, an exhausted Ontos crewman ignores discomfort to snatch twenty winks. *Official USMC Photo by Lance Corporal D. M. Messenger*

By the evening of February 21, everyone in the know was expressing the opinion that Hue would be liberated "in a matter of time," or "a few days, at most." It only remained to be seen how many more lives would be lost before the Communists acknowledged the obvious.

*

The NVA opened the February 22 fighting in the Citadel with a twenty-round mortar barrage at 0330 that targeted Bravo/1/5 and Charlie/1/5. Four Marines were killed and four were wounded. The Marines responded with their mortars, but no results could be observed. Also before dawn on February 22, Battle Group Alpha was struck by a vicious 122mm rocket barrage.

1/5 moved into the attack again at 0930, but the NVA were packed solidly into their defensive zone, and all three front-line companies were pretty much out of gas. The attack was desultory and the response was spotty.

At about noon, when word arrived at the 1/5 command post that Lima/3/5 was ready to join the fight, Major Thompson decided to relieve particularly hard-hit Bravo/1/5 and send its fifty or sixty survivors back to Phu Bai to recuperate.

At 1300, the Alpha/1/5 patrol crept out of the buildings next to the Thuong Tu Gate and made its way without opposition to the wall at the Citadel's eastern corner. There, Corporal James Avella pulled a small American flag from his pack. The implication was clear. Avella wired the flag to a thin metal pipe, climbed to the roof of a tin shed, and affixed the pipe to a telegraph pole.

Lima/3/5, supported by several M48 tanks, went into the attack as soon as it reached the 1/5 front line. Fueled by the valor of the uninitiated, the company swept forward into strongpoints 1/5 Marines no longer even dreamed of approaching in broad daylight. As the lead platoon rushed across a bridge it found in its path to the Citadel wall, NVA snipers concealed throughout the area initiated a devastating crossfire. A handful of the Lima/3/5 Marines were cut down, and many of the survivors were temporarily pinned down.

In midafternoon, even though the cloud level was too close to the ground for safe bombing runs, a pair of Marine jet attack bombers delivered bombs and napalm on NVA positions hard up against 1/5. They were credited with killing seventy-three NVA within 150 meters of the Citadel wall.

*

The fight in the Battle Group Alpha zone on February 22 began at 0645, when NVA atop and within the Citadel wall opened fire with machine guns and rifles. Mortars set in farther to the southeast added to the mayhem. Casualties mounted. At 0830, an NVA counterattack pushed part of a battalion of the 3d ARVN Regiment out of a schoolhouse it had been holding for days between the VNMC lines and the 1/5 sector.

Battle Group Alpha was again supported by creeping 8-inch howitzer barrages from the south. For each fire mission, the 8-inch registration rounds were placed on a line 300 meters southeast of the VNMC line, and then the subsequent all-out barrage was drawn closer in small increments until Vietnamese marines on the front line sent word that they were receiving shrapnel in their positions. Following each barrage, ARVN psychological-warfare loudspeakers were brought up and the NVA and VC facing the VNMC were given an opportunity to surrender. All or most of the Communist fighters remained in their bunkers and fighting holes, but they allowed hundreds of civilians to cross into the VNMC lines. No doubt, some NVA and VC fighters escaped in civilian disguise, but several were captured when they flunked interrogation or were turned in by civilians.

For all the artillery and propaganda barrages, the 4th and 5th VNMC battalions made no forward progress on February 22. The NVA and VC holding the Huu Gate open were, if anything, even more determined to hold than ever.

*

Victory was in the air in the 1/5 zone of action. Alpha/1/5's 2d Platoon had spent the night of February 22–23 atop the wall at the Citadel's eastern corner, and the NVA in the area made no hostile moves in its direction. At 0800, February 23, Delta/1/5 attacked from its line a block from the southeastern wall and punched through to the objective against sporadic sniper fire. Two Marines were wounded in the final assault.

When Delta/1/5 went into the attack toward the wall, the much larger Lima/3/5 pivoted to the southwest to attack toward the Imperial Palace's

Corporal James Avella, of Alpha/1/5, prepares to raise a small American flag over the Thuong Tu Gate. *Texas Tech Virtual Vietnam Archive*

A Delta/1/5 rifleman goes toe-to-toe with NVA riflemen on the other side of one of the few clear areas in the company's zone of action. *Official USMC Photo by Lance Corporal D. M. Messenger*

eastern corner. Few NVA faced the company, but those who did put up remarkably strong resistance. Initial progress was slow, no doubt partly because Lima/3/5's veterans of one day's city fighting played it safe. One of the two or three M48 tanks supporting Lima/3/5 was struck at 0945 by an RPG. One crewman was killed, one crewman was

Marines on the southern
bank of the Perfume
River fire at Communist
troops swarming out of
the Citadel following the
final Marine, ARVN, and
VNMC advances inside
the walled city. *Texas
Tech Virtual Vietnam
Archive*

back, it was struck by three more RPGs. Lima/3/5 Marines in the vicinity spotted the source of the RPGs, poured out a heavy volume of M16 and M60 fire, and called for a 60mm mortar mission. The NVA returned fire, but their position was quickly blotted out by the mortars. The tank completed its withdrawal unmolested, but one Lima/3/5 Marine was killed, six were wounded and evacuated, and five sustained minor wounds in the exchange.

At 1020, the main body of Alpha/1/5 was struck by three 82mm mortar rounds as it inched its way along the outside of the Imperial Palace's northeast wall. Four Marines were wounded and evacuated, and one injured Marine stayed with the company.

Early in the afternoon, as Delta/1/5 attacked to the southwest to clear NVA-held bunkers and passages within the southeastern wall itself, the lead element ran into a large, determined NVA force holed up in a series of interconnecting, mutually supporting bunkers and pillboxes. Extremely heavy fire from rifles, machine guns, and RPGs threatened to stop the Delta/1/5 drive, but Captain Myron Harrington was not in the mood to let anything stand between him and final victory in Hue. Harrington moved forward with a pair of 3.5-inch rocket teams and directed them against the cornerstone of the NVA defensive sector. Then he darted from front-line position to front-line position, pinpointing objectives for his troops and directing suppressive small-arms fire. As Harrington personally called artillery and mortar fire down to within 25 meters of his own position, four NVA front-line positions were overrun under his direct supervision. As the NVA defensive sector started to crack, Harrington worked his way forward, rallied his company's point elements, and personally led an assault on yet another NVA position. At that point Delta/1/5 began to make some serious headway through the crumbling NVA strongpoint. When the attack finally routed the NVA

lightly injured, and the heavily damaged tank had to be driven to the rear. Shortly, Lima/3/5 found its stride and delivered what Major Thompson called a "beautiful" attack. The sky was clear; there was plenty of air support. Lima/3/5 moved forward like a well-oiled machine. Two or three tanks and two Ontos attacked in perfect harmony with the infantry. In the course of the initial phase of the attack, Thuong Tu Gate finally fell securely into U.S. Marine hands.

One of the tanks supporting Lima/3/5 was struck by several RPGs fired from the Imperial Palace wall, and three crewmen were injured. A minute later, as the damaged tank was pulling force, Harrington's Marines counted twenty-five dead NVA soldiers within the strongpoint. Captain Myron Harrington was awarded a Navy Cross for his role in leading the attack.

At this point, 1/5 was in a position from which it could drive to the main Citadel flagpole. But that was an honor forbidden to any but a South Vietnamese unit. Thus 1/5 ended the day in possession of about all the objectives it could legally seize. Except for straightening its front line and mopping up throughout its rear, there was nothing left for 1/5 to do inside the Citadel of Hue.

*

The 4th and 5th VNMC battalions jumped off into their February 23 attack at 1100. An immense early-morning air and artillery bombardment had been promised against specific targets and large areas all along and well ahead of their fronts, but hours-long delays had led to no such support at all. Lacking support even from their own 81mm mortars, for which there was no ammunition, each battalion simply attacked with three companies abreast. Once again, the Vietnamese marines were unable to get across the Thuy Quan Canal. Repeated efforts by leaders to motivate the troops produced repeated attempts to breach the NVA front, but it was clear from the outset that Battle Group Alpha was going to get nowhere that day. By day's end, morale had plummeted, an unusual turn of events among normally stoic Vietnamese troops, and particularly so in the elite VNMC.

*

The end came before dawn on February 24.

General Truong ordered the 2d Battalion, 3d ARVN Regiment, to proceed along the top of the Citadel's southeastern wall from the Delta/1/5 line to the flagpole. The move was conducted in the wee hours, and the final assault was mounted at 0500. The ARVN troops killed thirty-one of the enemy soldiers and easily overran the objective.

At dawn, the huge NLF banner that had taunted and haunted South Vietnam's and

Triumphant ARVN soldiers celebrate their victory over the Communist invaders of Hue by raising their national colors on the 200-foot flag pole from which a Viet Cong flag has flown for twenty-four days. In clouds of colored smoke from grenades placed at the base of the pole, the huge flag of the Republic of Vietnam billows in a stiff breeze as soldiers prepare to hoist it to the top of the pole. Frustrated in their attempt to raise the flag when a halyard breaks, the determined South Vietnamese strap it to the backs of two soldiers who climb to the top and tie the flag where it can be seen from the entire city.
Texas Tech Virtual Vietnam Archive/Douglas Pike Photo Collection

America's political leaders since January 31 was hauled down by triumphant ARVN soldiers. Moments later, it was replaced with an equally large version of South Vietnam's national colors.

At 0730, the main body of the somewhat recuperated 3d ARVN Regiment, bolstered by a troop of the 7th ARVN Armored Cavalry Battalion, advanced to the Imperial Palace's outer walls against spotty resistance. To the accompaniment of patriotic music broadcast over loudspeakers, the ARVN soldiers thoroughly shot up the palace wall and hurled hand grenades over the top. By 1025, the last shred of hostile fire had been subdued. At that point, General Truong ordered the Hoc Bao

Official USMC Photo by Sergeant William L. Dickman

The bodies of many NVA soldiers were unearthed or uncovered during precautionary sweeps through fallen bunkers and fortified houses. *Official USMC Photos by Lance Corporal D. M. Messenger*

ARVN soldiers raise their national colors on a makeshift flagstaff over the Thuong Tu Gate. *Official USMC Photo by Lance Corporal D. M. Messenger*

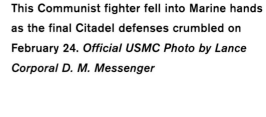

This Communist fighter fell into Marine hands as the final Citadel defenses crumbled on February 24. *Official USMC Photo by Lance Corporal D. M. Messenger*

Marine riflemen, well on the road to recovery from their ordeal, playfully model Communist headgear liberated in the wake of the Citadel battle. *Official USMC Photo by Lance Corporal D. M. Messenger*

Delta/1/5 Marines and ARVN soldiers freely walk the street leading to the Thuong Tu Gate. *Official USMC Photo by Staff Sergeant Jack Harlan*

The Emperor of Hue. This Marine sergeant momentarily occupies the imperial throne following the liberation of the Imperial Palace. *Official USMC Photo by Staff Sergeant Jack Harlan*

Company, the 1st ARVN Division Reconnaissance Company, and the 2d Battalion, 3d ARVN Regiment, to kick open the Imperial Palace's Ngo Mon Gate and secure the interior. More preparatory gunfire and grenade-throwing ensued, but the attack finally got under way at 1515. At 1700 the Imperial Palace was declared secure.

Throughout the morning, Battle Group Alpha moved once again to breach the NVA defenses along the Thuy Quan Canal. As soon as the attack jumped off, it became obvious that many NVA soldiers had been withdrawn or had simply abandoned their positions. The vital Huu Gate was secured before noon by two companies of the 4th VNMC Battalion, and the two-battalion attack quickly advanced beyond it. Any NVA or VC remaining inside the Citadel were trapped there. The Vietnamese marines were unable to complete the attack to the Citadel's southern corner by sunset, but they jumped off again at 0500, February 25, and, with the help of two U.S. Marine Ontos, the southern corner fell in very short order.

EPILOGUE

The city of Hue was declared secure by I ARVN Corps headquarters on February 26, 1968. For all the official news marking "the end" of the battle, bloody combat operations in and around Hue continued against stubborn Communist units and stragglers for, in some places, three weeks.

Of the three U.S. Marine battalions committed to combat in Hue, Lieutenant Colonel Mark Gravel's 1/1 continued to run security patrols in the area east of MACV until it was relieved in early March. Lieutenant Colonel Ernie Cheatham's 2/5, which had liberated the modern city center as far as the Phu Cam Canal by February 10, just about destroyed the main body of the 4th NVA Regiment in aggressive sweep and pursuit operations south of the canal through the end of February. Then 2/5 and Major Bob Thompson's 1/5 conducted sweep and security operations between the Perfume River and the South China Sea during the first few days of March. Task Force X-Ray declared the end of

Operation Hue City on March 2. On March 4, 1/5 was transferred back to 5th Marines and ordered to Phu Bai to refit. On March 5, Colonel Stan Hughes and his staff left MACV to return to Phu Bai. On March 8, 2/5 moved south to begin a new operation under the direction of 5th Marines.

Throughout the period following the fall of the Citadel, the 2d Brigade of the 101st Airborne Division and the 3d Brigade of the 1st Cavalry Division continued to sweep toward the city from the north and west. They and other elements of both U.S. Army divisions crossed the Perfume River and conducted mop-up operations for several days. Then the U.S. Army units were withdrawn to undertake operations that had been planned before the Tet emergency broke.

Battle Group Alpha also remained in contact with Communist units and stragglers in and around Hue. When it was withdrawn in early March, the three VNMC battalions were returned

The 1st Platoon, Alpha/1/1, on the day it left Hue. An estimated fifty Marines and corpsman, including replacements, served in this platoon during February 1968. Counting casualties returned to duty, twenty left under their own power.
Courtesy of Sergeant Major Eddie Neas

to their southern cantonments to re-equip and train replacements for the hundreds of Vietnamese marines killed and wounded in Saigon and Hue.

The 1st ARVN Division, which was home-based in Hue, continued to mop up in and around the city, but it slowly went back to its previous routine of sweeping around and across northern I Corps. It took many months to get the division back to its pre-Tet strength, and months longer to effectively absorb and train the new conscripts. For all that, as long as the division benefited from the stalwart leadership of Brigadier General Ngo Quang Truong, it prospered as one of the best of the ARVN combat divisions.

In the end, beautiful Hue lay in ruins. Years of rebuilding lay ahead, and the job was far from complete when the Republic of Vietnam fell before the final NVA offensive in 1975. The real tragedy of the battle for Hue lay not in the physical damage, nor even in the loss of national treasures, but in the deaths of many hundreds of Hue's citizens—the unfortunate random deaths and maimings in the battles to liberate the city, and in the nearly two thousand documented cases of mass murder and execution that claimed the lives of many of the city's—and the nation's—leading businessmen, government workers, politicians, theologians, foreign missionaries and doctors, intellectuals, and teachers. This brutal human toll—discovered in many unmarked individual and mass graves located over a period of months and years—was the one from which neither the city nor the nation ever rebounded. In a way, the unified nation of Vietnam is still paying a colossal price for the irredeemable acts of the Communist hit squads.

After the Fall

Refugees live beneath these scraps of cardboard and tin. *Official USMC Photo*

Official USMC Photo

Witnesses told investigators of seeing more than 300 civilians force-marched from the Catholic Diocese of Phu Cam on February 5, 1968, under heavy guard. The prisoners' hands were bound behind their backs with wire and the prisoners were linked to one another by lengths of wire. Many were women and children. Examination of the remains of the as many as 250 victims found in just one mass grave indicated that many were clubbed to death and some were shot. Records at Hue showed that at least 3,000 people were reported missing after the twenty-five-day occupation of the city by Communists. More than 2,000 bodies were discovered in more than two dozen mass graves. *Texas Tech Virtual Vietnam Archive/Douglas Pike Photo*

Remains of a family killed in their home in the Citadel. They were most likely inadvertent battle casualties. *Official USMC Photo by Lance Corporal D. M. Messenger*

The bodies of German medical instructors abducted by a Communist hit squad from Hue University were recovered from an unmarked grave. Note that their hands are bound behind their backs. *Texas Tech Virtual Vietnam Archive/Douglas Pike Photo Collection*

Official USMC Photo

ARVN Lieutenant Le Kim Ngoc (left) holds the paper lining of the casket as his father, who was arrested and assassinated by Viet Cong in Hue on February 8, 1968, is laid to rest in a proper burial. *Texas Tech Virtual Vietnam Archive/Douglas Pike Photo Collection*

Official USMC Photo

The Imperial Palace. *Official USMC*

A church in southern Hue. *Official USMC Photo by Sergeant William L. Dickman*

Buddhist women mourn the dead. *Texas Tech Virtual Vietnam Archive/Douglas Pike Photo Collection*

Official USMC Photo

Regional and Popular Forces troops load victims found in a mass grave for transportation to a mortuary site in the city. *Texas Tech Virtual Vietnam Archive*

Displaced innocents.

Official USMC Photo by Master Sergeant C. F. X. Houts

Official USMC Photo by Lance Corporal Gustav Hasford

Colonel Chuck Meadows Collection

HamiltonBook.com

Falls Village, CT 06031-5010 – *service@hamiltonbook.com*

03660478
Laurel & Richard Cosbie
73225 Bursera Way
Palm Desert CA 92260-5705

885877837   BATCH 16931092

ORDER RECEIVED: 1/19/2015

ITEMS SHIPPED: 9

9

12-19

THE FOLLOWING ITEMS HAVE BEEN SHIPPED:

1-37	1 01X2-C	Jump Commander: In Combat with the 505th	4.95	7566611
1-33	1 03S2-C	Pacific War Uncensored: A War Correspond	9.95	5599199
0-71	1 11D0-P	Fighting for the French Foreign Legion	13.95	6512089
1-24	1 12D2-P	Danger's Hour: The Story of the USS Bunk	3.95	6503047
0-99	1 16D1-C	Voices of the Pacific: Untold Stories fr	7.95	7585500
1-53	1 50T1-P	Best War Stories Ever Told	5.95	5491827
1-46	1 55W1-C	Burma 1942: The Road from Rangoon to Man	5.95	7581475
0-98	1 62D1-P	Depths of Courage: American Submariners	4.95	4505700
2-58	1 65V4-C	Marines in Hue City: A Portrait of Urban	3.95	7582234

Your credit card will be charged for the items shipped.
If any items were not shipped, a second shipment will be made as soon as possible, but in no case later than 60 days.
You will be charged for those items when they are shipped. You will be notified if any items are not available.

If you receive a damaged, defective, or incorrect item please do NOT return it. Just let us know what is wrong and we will correct it.
You may return any item for a refund of its purchase price. You pay only the postage.

POPULAR TITLES THAT MAY INTEREST YOU

DVD THE KOREAN WAR: 60th Anniversary.
This collection of documentary footage chronicles the roots of the conflict as it blossomed into a protracted war that took a heavy toll in American blood and treasure. The immediacy of combat and major conflicts are brought to vivid life in over 16 hours of dramatic documentaries and footage. In Color and B&W. Over 22 hours on four DVDs. Mill Creek.
Item #5617723   Published at $9.98   **$5.95**

THE BOOK OF BASIC MACHINES: The U.S. Navy Training Manual.
Have you ever wondered why levers and pulleys make it easy to lift heavy objects, or thought what makes a combustion engine work? This reference will give you all the information you need to understand such key mechanical concepts, techniques, and components. Drawings. Skyhorse. Paperbound.
Item #7528795   Published at $12.95   **$4.95**

U.S. ARMY IMPROVISED MUNITIONS HANDBOOK.
This handbook describes in detail how to build munitions from seemingly harmless materials that can be bought at drug or paint stores, found in junk piles, or acquired from military stocks. Features explanations of how to construct explosives, detonators, propellants, incendiaries, delays, and more. 600+ illus. 251 pages. Skyhorse. Paperbound.
Item #4290402   Published at $12.95   **$5.95**

DVD WINGS OF GLORY: The Official Story of the Air Force.
Fullscreen. Witness the growth of the Air Force over the years through authentic archival footage filmed by American combat cameramen. Discover how the Air Force grew from a few daring men to a force with capabilities beyond the wildest dreams of the early aviation visionaries. In Color and B&W. Over 6 hours on three DVDs. Timeless Media Group.
Item #7594100   Published at $29.98   **$3.95**

MILITARY MISDEMEANORS: Corruption, Incompetence, Lust, and Downright Stupidity. By Terry Crowdy. Tells tales of the cat-eating soldier, philandering emperors, the transvestite spy, satanic masses aboard ship, a 20th-century witchcraft trial, Britain's opium abuse, stolen babies, and mutiny on the high seas. 320 pages. Osprey.
Item #7524935   Published at $16.95   **$2.95**

DVD CENTURY OF WARFARE.
Fullscreen. This set documents America's rise to the most powerful military nation in the world, from horse-drawn cannons in WWI to the laser-guided missiles of Desert Storm. Covers WWI, WWII, The Korean War, The Vietnam War, and Operation Desert Storm. In Color and B&W. Six hours on 3 DVDs. Timeless Media Group.
Item #6468349   **$3.95**

DVD WARBIRDS OVER THE TRENCHES.
Fullscreen. Presents a compelling 5-part look at air combat in the First World War. Includes captivating final interviews with some of the men who flew in the Great War, incredible archival film footage, and video of restored aircraft still flying 100 years later. In Color and B&W. Over 4 hours on two DVDs. Mill Creek.
Item #7546246   Published at $9.98   **$5.95**

SOLDATEN: On Fighting, Killing, and Dying.
By S. Neitzel & H. Welzer. The authors examine reams of untouched, recently declassified transcripts of covert recordings of German POWs. These extraordinary bugged conversations reveal through the eyes of German soldiers the often brutal reality of the Second World War. 437 pages. Knopf.
Item #6520227   Published at $30.50   **$5.95**

THE RISE AND FALL OF THE THIRD REICH: A History of Nazi Germany. By William L. Shirer. An abridged edition of the most familiar account of Hitler's regime, its horrific adventures and its sensational destruction, woven with a wealth of archival photographs that make the story all the more palpable. Book Club Edition. 50 photos, some color. 1249 pages. S&S. 9x11¾.
Item #7585055   **$7.95**

CODE NAME CAESAR: The Secret Hunt for U-Boat 864 During World War II. By J. Preisler & K. Sewell. As the Allies pressed forward in Europe and the Pacific in the days of WWII, a little-known battle took place under the frozen seas off the coast of Norway. It was a battle that would change the course of the war. This dramatic account documents that unsung moment in the annals of naval warfare. Photos. 287 pages. Berkley.
Item #5615542   Published at $26.95   **$5.95**

I WAS HITLER'S PILOT: The Memoirs of Hans Baur.
First published in 1958, this is a compelling account written by one of the few members of the inner circle to survive the final days in the Berlin bunker and the last man to see Martin Bormann alive. It gives insights into Hitler's private thoughts, daily activities, and conversations. Book Club Edition. Photos. 243 pages. Frontline. Import.
Item #7576846   Originally Published at $29.95   **$3.95**

THE RANGER FORCE: Darby's Rangers in World War II.
By Robert W. Black. Alongside the Flying Tigers and the Devil's Brigade, the U.S. 6615th Ranger Force–better known as Darby's Rangers–ranks among the most famous fighting formations of WWII. In this action-packed account, Black draws on years of original research to reconstruct their combat history. Illus. 418 pages. Stackpole.
Item #6496768   Published at $29.95   **$6.95**

KILL ANYTHING THAT MOVES: The Real American War in Vietnam.
By Nick Turse. Drawing on more than a decade of research in secret Pentagon files and interviews with American veterans and Vietnamese survivors, Turse reveals how official policies resulted in millions of innocent civilians killed and wounded, and how they made crimes in almost every combat unit inevitable. Photos. 370 pages. Metropolitan.
Item #7565798   Published at $30.00   **$6.95**

PAPA BRAVO ROMEO: U.S. Navy Patrol Boats at War in Vietnam.
By Wynn Goldsmith. Presents a river rat's graphic, harrowing account of fighting in the Viet Cong-infested Mekong Delta. Photos. 285 pages. Ballantine. Paperbound.
Item #7661827   Published at $6.99   **$2.95**

FIGHTING TO LEAVE: The Final Years of America's War in Vietnam, 1972-1973. By Robert E. Stoffey. Covers the Vietnam War during 1972-73, the tumultuous final years of U.S. involvement, as experienced by Col. Stoffey, a Marine Corps aviator who served three tours in Vietnam. Stoffey offers a unique perspective on the end of America's war in Vietnam. Photos. 336 pages. Zenith.
Item #5519896   Published at $25.95   **$3.95**

LAST STAND AT KHE SANH: The U.S. Marines' Finest Hour in Vietnam. By Gregg Jones. Drawing on in-depth interviews with siege survivors, archival documents, and scores of oral history accounts, Jones delivers a poignant and heartpounding narrative of the 1968 siege of Khe Sanh, when 6,000 U.S. Marines awoke one January morning to find themselves surrounded by 20,000 enemy troops. 16 pages of photos. 358 pages. Da Capo.
Item #6507468   Published at $26.99   **$16.95**

THE BATTLE FOR SAIGON: Tet 1968.
By Keith William Nolan. Intense and in-depth look at the Tet Offensive, the most pivotal battle of the Vietnam war, from its cemetery firefights to roof-top shootouts. Photos. 274 pages. Presidio. Paperbound.
Item #7560524   Published at $17.95   **$3.95**

TRUE FAITH AND ALLEGIANCE: An American Paratrooper and the 1972 Battle for An Loc. By Mike McDermott. At once an account of brutal infantry warfare and a critique of the mishandling of America's departure from Indochina, this gripping in-the-trenches narrative recounts the grueling battle for An Loc, as seen through the eyes of a senior advisor to an elite South Vietnamese paratrooper battalion. Illus. 188 pages. UAIP.
Item #7521707   **$5.95**

Index